A Rose for Reuben

A Rose for...

A Rose for Reuben

Stories of Hope from the Holocaust

Robert Rietti

For Colette.

In admiration,

Robert (Rietti)

CANTERBURY
PRESS
Norwich

© Robert Rietti 2006

First published in 2006 by the Canterbury Press Norwich
(a publishing imprint of Hymns Ancient & Modern
Limited, a registered charity)
9–17 St Albans Place, London N1 0NX

www.scm-canterburypress.co.uk

British Library Cataloguing in Publication data

A catalogue record for this book is available
from the British Library

ISBN 1-85311-674-2
9781-85311-674-2

Typeset by Regent Typesetting, London
Printed and bound by
Bookmarque, Croydon, Surrey

For Tina

'How do I love thee? Let me count the ways:
I love thee to the depth and breadth and height
My soul can reach.'

Elizabeth Browning,
Sonnets from the Portuguese
Sonnet 43

Contents

vii

CONTENTS

About the Author

Robert Rietti comes from a distinguished Italian family dating back to the thirteenth century, when one of his ancestors was physician to the pope and who performed the first known blood transfusion, on the pontiff.

Robert has had a varied career as an actor, director, playwright and broadcaster. He has also been responsible for dubbing many successful foreign films into English and specializes in re-voicing artistes and completing the sound-track of English-made pictures in which foreign artistes have also been used and whose accents may need correcting or replacing. He was nominated for the Golden Reel Award in Hollywood for his dubbing of *Once Upon a Time in America*. He also won the Oxford Film Festival Award for 'The best foreign film in the English language' with his version of the Russian film *Pavlova* and in 2000 was nominated for the BAFTA Special Award for Outstanding Work. After Jack Hawkins had lost the use of his voice through throat cancer, Robert undertook to imitate him and to record his dialogue in his last ten films.

He has broadcast over 6,000 times and for over six years recorded a weekly programme from the BBC to the United States, as their answer to Alistair Cooke's *Letter from America*. His reading of D. H. Lawrence's *Rocking Horse Winner* won such acclaim that the recording was awarded the rare privilege of being buried in the BBC archives for future generations.

Members of the Rietti family came to Britain 200 years

ago and the grandmother of Benjamin Disraeli (British Prime Minister) was Rebecca Rietti.

In 1988 the Italian Government honoured him with the title of 'Cavaliere al Merito' (Knighthood of Merit) for his services to the Italian theatre and films. In 1990 this title was up-graded to 'Officer Knight of the Italian Republic'.

Robert is the founder and editor of the British drama quarterly called *Gambit*. He has translated many plays from Italian and is at present embarked on publishing the entire dramatic works of Luigi Pirandello into English commissioned by the publisher John Calder. The first five volumes are already on the market.

Foreword

It is a privilege and a pleasure to have been asked to write the Foreword to *A Rose for Reuben* by Robert Rietti. It is a book that reflects Robert's generous, caring and charming personality. It reveals his deep commitment to Judaism and to his family, particularly his wife Tina.

The book is a collection of stories. The stories are all short; the longest is only eight pages. Each story is complete in itself, but it is their combined impact that is so effective. They are all linked directly or indirectly to the dreadful events that took place during the Holocaust. In these circumstances, it is inevitable that the stories have their tragic and horrendous aspects. However, each of them leaves you uplifted. They are a testament as to how goodness can come out of evil. Each story has its hero who demonstrates human nature at its best. They may have had to be persuaded to tell their tale. But the story tellers in every case have immensely rich and warm personalities. They are also extraordinarily modest. They demonstrate how it is possible to cope with adversity, cast aside bitterness and be enriched by the most terrible experiences. The stories renew your faith in human nature.

It is indeed fortunate that Robert was able to coax so many of the Holocaust survivors he met to tell their stories, to make it possible to record them in this book. In a few years time the stories would have been lost forever. This would have been a tragedy because in Robert's hands they together provide such wonderful and deeply moving book.

For someone with Robert's deep feeling for Judaism the stories have an extra dimension. However, even those who do not share Robert's strong faith will find they are uplifted by them. Certainly I was and found the experience of reading them totally inspiring. Any one like myself, who has not a deep sense of faith, will be left pondering the remarkable sets of circumstances that resulted in loved ones being reunited in the most extraordinary of circumstances. Coincidence, or the hand of fate, or the work of some divine being, you must come to your own conclusion. Whatever is your answer you will have found this book fascinating. I hope these stories reach a very wide audience. The audience will, in turn, be horrified, humbled, amused and inspired.

A *Rose for Reuben* takes only a short time to read, and every minute spent doing so will be well spent. I earnestly hope that there are many more stories to be told and that we can look forward to a sequel.

Lord Woolf

Introduction

For many years I have had a niche in religious and inspirational programmes for BBC Radio and Television and Scottish Television and these have resulted in very many letters from listeners asking if my talks have been published and, if so, where the book can be obtained. The following is a selection from those talks plus others not yet broadcast. My thanks are due to Toby Horton of Heritage Media who organized and produced my recent series of programmes for Radio 4 with great expertise and efficiency and to the numerous people from whom I have gleaned their remarkable stories. Some of those events will have been told and retold till they have almost entered the realm of legend. Each storyteller will have coloured them in his or her own style – but all versions will have the merit of being true events which inspire and help to renew one's faith in the One above who listens and observes and who DOES answer even though we may not always recognize His hand in the resolution to our problems.

A few years ago I was privileged to work closely with Marcel Ophuls on two of his remarkable documentaries of the last war and Nazi atrocities – *The Sorrow and the Pity* and *Memory of Justice* – and from this genius of filmmaking I learned a most useful lesson. When interviewing war criminals he would talk to them for days, gaining their confidence and overcoming their reluctance to answer him directly. Having broken the ice, he would ask a series of seemingly innocuous questions, then suddenly throw in a leading question, and before he realized it, the man found himself giving away information he had been attempting to hide.

When interviewing Holocaust survivors I often met with reluctance to talk of their ghastly experiences. Applying Marcel's technique, I would spend hours, if not days, putting them at their ease until – suddenly – the flood-gates opened and they poured forth the amazing events I have recounted in the following pages. In many cases those survivors had tried to close the doors of memory and never told their children of their sufferings in the death camps. One thing struck me: those scarred men and women appeared to have no rancour, no desire for revenge. They recounted the most horrendous events in a quiet, unsensational manner, as though they are somehow detached from the personal experience and were able to talk of terrifying experiences without sentimentality or sensationalism. Surprisingly they appeared to have found their faith in God had been strengthened rather than diminished by what had happened to them. I expected to hear recriminations, blame thrust upon the Almighty for the ghastly happenings – but instead I found a philosophical acceptance, looking forward rather than dwelling on the past, attributing the miracle of their survival to His magnanimity. I found gratitude in their hearts to the Father of mankind for guiding them through the valley of death, surrounding them with His protecting hand. They exuded a humanity and compassion and often even forgiveness and sadness, but a gentle acceptance and quiet dignity shone from them. It was as though they had taken to heart the age old Jewish maxim, 'This too has to be for the best.'

One poignant account I came across will remain in my mind for ever. Aharon Appelfeld described a group of blind children, dressed in their sabbath best, being marched from the Institute for the Blind to the local railway station to be deported to the camps. The children began to sing songs by Schubert and Bach as well as Yiddish and folk songs. When they reached the station, the Ukrainian guards began to beat them with their clubs – but the children still managed to sing their anthem in its entirety before being thrown into the cattle trucks to be transported to their deaths.

The men and women I interviewed granted me permission to write and tell about their experiences, but some extracted from me the promise that I would not reveal their real names. In humility and admiration I ask my readers to share with me these remarkable events.

Thanks go to Yitta Halberstam, Judith Leventhal, Chaim Walder, Yaffa Eliach, Hanoch Teller and so many others whose painstaking research and personal memories of the Holocaust have proved an inspiration to us all.

> 'True stories are meant to be passed on.
> To keep them to oneself is to betray them.'
> Elie Wiesel

A Rose for Reuben

More than half a century has passed since millions of innocent Jews, political prisoners and Gypsies perished in the
Nazi death camps. The statistics are not to be forgotten.
Over six million Jews, two million Polish Catholics, half a
million Gypsies, seven hundred thousand Serbian Orthodox
Christians, one hundred and fifty thousand Germans who
were political or religious opponents or handicapped, as
well as three million Russian prisoners of war were killed in
concentration and transit camps that stretched from France
to Ukraine. We understand too well the suffering those
individuals experienced, but what of those who survived
the massacres and other vicissitudes in life and who –
through faith, inner belief, optimism, wondrous hope in the
midst of despair – have learned to rejoin the broken threads
of their lives – never to forget – but perhaps to forgive?

There are countless tales of how happiness has replaced
the misery of those tortuous years, but there are some for
whom fate has reserved an unexpected blow. Let me tell
you what happened to my friend, Reuben.

At times, when I was an out-of-work young actor, I took on
other temporary jobs. Once I worked in a soap factory
where the unforgiving hours were spent filling paper bags
with soap powder which irritated the eyes and nose and
encouraged a constant sneeze. Another time I trudged sub-
urban streets, knocking at countless doors, demonstrating a
new water-softener to uninterested housewives. Smiling

with simulated ecstasy, I drank innumerable glasses of soft water without selling one machine. Yet another time I worked for a tailor in the East End of London, sewing lining in boys' schoolcaps. It was not a difficult task and I enjoyed the mixed company. It was a family business run on very old-fashioned lines, and Mr Marks, the tailor, firmly put into practice his belief that what machines can do, human fingers do better.

It was a particularly warm summer, I remember, and one stifling evening I came home from work feeling exhausted. I changed my clothes and sat down panting by the window of my bed-sitting room when there was a knock at the door. Before I could reply it was flung open and a woman walked in. She was short and fat, untidy in her dress, and had dyed blonde hair imprisoned in curlers. Her sleeves were rolled up and she held a ladle in her hand which swung away and against her like a pendulum.

'I am Reuben's wife!' she said aggressively.

I must explain that Reuben lived in the same block of flats, and although I had known him only to greet with a passing 'good morning' or 'good evening', it was he who came to my rescue when the rent was too overdue to be comfortable. Reuben worked for Mr Marks, the tailor, and he put in a good word to his employer who then gave me that part-time and very welcome job. The blonde woman looked at me quite menacingly and began to gesture with her ladle in a rather dangerous manner. I offered her a chair, but she shook her head – and in order to create some distance between us, I took the proffered chair myself.

'Look here,' she said, 'how is it I see you come home from work with all other respectable peoples and mine husband not? Huh? And it's not the first time either that he's gone goodness knows where and come home two hours after everyone else. Where's he loitering about?'

'I don't know,' I said.

'Ah . . . so you don't know! What do you mean by that?! Don't you leave the workshop together? Eh? Is he so thin that you can't see him? Does he grow wings with which to fly? How can you not help seeing what becomes of my man?'

I thought back a moment, remembering that when Reuben and I left the tailor's, he sometimes walked a little way with me, usually in silence and then turned off in another direction, and that one day when I asked where he was going, he had replied 'To . . . to see some friends.'

I avoided quoting Reuben and put it to her as a suggestion on my part. The woman laughed. 'Friends?! We are foreigners, we are, we have no friends! What friends should he have, poor miserable wretch! Huh! Friends! If that's what he told you it's just to blink mine eyes! I'll teach him a lesson he won't forget in a hurry!' And with that she stormed out of my room. I pictured to myself poor consumptive Reuben being 'taught a lesson' by his angry wife, and I pitied him.

From the window I watched her cross the little grass patch, flatteringly known as the gardens, between the two entrances to the apartments and enter her block, slamming the door violently. A window pane that had already been cracked and held together with Sellotape gave up the ghost and shattered into many small pieces. I took a pan and brush and went out to sweep up the mess before any child could get hurt.

Reuben was still in his thirties but you would not have believed it. His sallow face was set in a straggly beard. He was extraordinarily thin, always ailing and coughing: a quiet man . . . simple, yet dignified. I might almost say the only one in the shop who never grudged a fellow-worker his livelihood. He had not been in England long . . . he and his wife had come from Germany as Holocaust survivors – and the others at work made fun of him because of his

3

accent. But I always stood up for him because I liked him very much. In his quiet, unobtrusive way he had become almost a necessity to the smooth running of the workshop. It was an odd thing that whenever one of the others was in trouble or needed advice, of all the people working there on whom he or she could have unburdened themselves, it was invariably Reuben who was singled out. Perhaps the secret lay in his ability to listen with his complete attention: as though your troubles were actually his, and the most important thing in the world at that moment was for him to share them with you.

After his aggressive wife had visited me I wondered to myself where he was disappearing to, and I resolved to find out.

The next morning, I met Reuben as usual, and at first I intended to tell him of his wife's visit to me the evening before, but the poor man looked so low-spirited, so thoroughly unhappy, that I felt certain his wife had already given him the 'promised lesson' and I hadn't the courage to mention her to him just then.

It was Reuben himself who first broached the subject. As we strolled away from the workshop at the end of the day he asked: 'Did my wife come to see you yesterday?'

'Yes, Reuben. She seemed annoyed with you.'

'Yes . . . she has a dreadful temper. When she's really angry she's fit to kill a man. But it's her bitter heart, poor thing. She's had so many troubles! She lost all her family in the gas chambers. She asked you where I go other days after work? Would you like to know? Come along with me and I'll show you.'

We walked on together and presently Reuben turned off the main road and led me into a narrow street not yet entirely built in with houses. A few more yards and he stopped with a contented smile. I looked around in some astonishment. We were standing by a piece of waste-ground with a meagre fencing of stones and wire and utilized as a garden.

'Just look,' said Reuben, 'how delightful it is. We hardly ever see anything like it where we live.' He went nearer to the fence and his eyes wandered thirstily over the flowering plants just then in full beauty.

I also looked at the garden. The plants that grew there were unknown to me and I was ignorant of their names. Only one thing had a familiar look: a few tall, graceful sunflowers were scattered here and there, and stood like absent-minded dreamers or beautiful sentinels. The roses were in bloom and their fragrance came in wafts over the fencing.

'Do you see those Paul Meyer roses?' Reuben asked in rapt tones, more to himself than to me. 'How beautiful they are. I can't take mine eyes off them. I can stand and look at them for hours. They make me feel happy – almost as if I were at home again in Munich. We had a lot of them at home.' He sighed, lost himself in thought a moment, then continued: 'We had quite a large garden and when the flowers began to come out, I used to sit there for hours and could never look at them enough. The flowers were all colours: pink and blue and yellow, and I felt as if everything were alive . . . as though the whole garden were alive. I fancied I heard them talking to each other . . . the roses, the geraniums, the honeysuckle. I spent whole evenings in my garden. It was dear to me as mine own soul. Look . . . look . . . don't the roses look as though they are alive!'

But I looked at Reuben and I thought the consumptive capmaker had grown younger and healthier. His face was less livid and his eyes shone with happiness.

'Do you know,' he said, 'I had some roses at the flat, in a window box, and they had begun to bud.'

There was a pause. 'Well,' I enquired, 'what happened?'

'Lisle . . . my wife . . . laid out the mattress to air on top of the box . . . and they were all crushed.'

Reuben made an outward gesture with his hand and I asked no more questions. For a long moment he stood still, gazing enraptured at the waste-ground: a lonely picture of a man who loved delicate and beautiful things, tied for life to an embittered, harsh, dominating woman who would never, never understand him.

On the way home he told me cheering news. It seemed that under the post-war reparations scheme of the new German government he was entitled to financial compensation for the compulsory sequestration of his family property by the Nazis and for the years spent in concentration camps. It was a substantial sum – some £8,000. It had been a long time coming and there was still no sign of it, but when it finally arrived he intended to use it to fulfil his greatest ambition: to open a florist's shop and to live every working hour of the day among the things he loved most in life.

Soon after that I was offered a job in a repertory company in the provinces, and I left London. I often wondered what became of Reuben, but on the one occasion I did write to him, my letter was returned with the words: 'Not known at this address'. A year or so later I was back in London and I decided to try and trace my old friend and to pay him a visit. On arriving at the block of flats where we had both lived I was astonished to find it partially demolished and rebuilding in progress. I enquired after Reuben – and the news completely stunned me. It appears that he had returned home from work one evening to find the building on fire and his screaming wife trapped in their top floor flat. Before the firemen could offer effective help, Reuben had climbed the five flights of stairs and forced his way through the flames, which had already devoured part of the landing and the entrance to his flat. Had his wife had the courage to return with him, all might have been well, but she was hysterical and refused to budge. By the time the blaze was under control, little was left of the entire floor, and the bodies of Reuben and his wife were found behind a wardrobe that had given them temporary shelter. Their arms were embraced in death as they had perhaps seldom been in life.

I took it upon myself to enquire whether they had any dependants or relatives who should have been informed of their demise, but there were none. They were strangers when they arrived in this country – and they were strangers when they died. What I did find out was that with the irony true of fate, shortly after the fire, news had arrived from Germany that all formalities had finally been cleared and Reuben's £8,000 compensation was now at his disposal.

He will never know how close he came to realizing his dream.

It is a habit of mine to take home a bunch of flowers to my wife every weekend and, although she had never met him, each time she selects one single rose to place in a vase on its own, as she says:

'This is for Reuben.'

A Billion to One

If I had not met him myself I might never have believed his story. It began in Warsaw in 1939 when the city was over-run by the Nazis. Moshe Czernaski was a young bank clerk, happily married to an attractive girl of his own age, Rebecca, and they had a fair-haired daughter called Katya.

Warsaw suffered greatly at the hands of its conquerors, and perhaps the hardest hit were the Jews. Moshe and his family were herded with the others into the Ghetto to be starved out of existence.

One day, coming back to their single room, Moshe found it deserted. In their periodic 'round-up' the Germans had cordoned off the block, ordered everyone on to the street and marched them off to the sealed cattle trucks which took them to the concentration camp. Moshe did not hear again of his wife and child. He joined the underground force and fought in the last stand of the Ghetto. He survived the massacre, the enslavement, the extermination, and finally regained his freedom with the liberation of Poland.

For months he searched for his family. For months he made every possible enquiry through the Red Cross and the Polish and German camps. Nothing. Then he met a man who claimed to have seen his wife and child in Auschwitz. The man said they had met their death in the gas chamber. Moshe closed that chapter of his life. He couldn't any longer bear the city that held so many memories, so he journeyed to America. There he changed his name to Maurice Korwin, rebuilt his life and prospered. When he was 50 he was enviably successful and respected by the staff of the business he had created in Boston.

He had no photo of his loved ones, but locked in his heart was the memory of a girl of 22 whose smile was like the sunlight, and a fair-headed child whose laughter still echoed in his mind. One day – acting on impulse – he packed a bag and flew to Israel. He joined the sightseers at the tomb of David, he visited other holy places and he saw how men had reclaimed the desert and turned it into a fertile land. But every fair face and every eager laugh tore at a deep wound within him till he could no longer recall the features of his loved ones, and every new face was their face and every new voice was their voice.

In Jerusalem he met a new immigrant who spoke only Polish. They liked each other and spent many happy hours together. She would not talk about her past life: she lived only for tomorrow. Like most new arrivals she had adopted a Hebrew name: Naomi. Soon Maurice realized that if he returned to Boston, neither his prosperous business nor his comfortable way of life could make up for his newly awakened feelings for Naomi – and so Maurice plucked up courage and posed the question. Naomi was touched. This older man who treated her with such tenderness and respect seemed to offer her the strength and purpose she most needed to start a new life. She too felt drawn to him and she accepted his proposal of marriage on one condition: that her mother should join them first. Now this was no easy task for Naomi herself had left Poland through underground channels. But wheels were set in motion, the right cogs were 'oiled' and eventually her mother managed to leave the country. Maurice went with Naomi to meet her at Haifa.

On the quayside he shared her excitement when she saw her mother. As the two fell into each other's arms, his pleasure in their reunion was not without its tinge of envy.

At last Naomi freed herself from her mother and introduced Maurice. The older woman studied him closely – then she turned pale. She said:

'Moshe . . . it's you!'

'Rebecca . . . Rebecca . . .!'

Slowly his arms outstretched – and man and wife held each other in a tight embrace for the first time in 26 years.

A billion to one chance wouldn't you say?

Chance? I wonder!

No Back Door

In the year 1934 Radawiec, west of Lublin in Poland, suffered a devastating fire and the entire town was burnt to the ground. It was not long before the resourceful inhabitants had managed to rebuild their homes – with one exception: Reb Pesach and his wife had lived with their children and grandchildren in a little cottage, earning a meagre living running a little store where they sold vegetables and the odd kitchen utensils. To be more precise, Reb Pesach's wife ran the store while her husband spent most of his days studying Jewish Law and poring over learned books written by his illustrious ancestors. He refused to have his cottage rebuilt as he maintained that 'man does not need property . . . it causes only hardship and worries. We can be quite content living in rented rooms.' His wife Lieb however was determined to have her own home again and sold the ground to a builder on condition that, in addition to a new house for himself, he would rebuild her cottage.

Most houses in Radawiec were constructed in wood and Lieb woke one morning to find that the builder had worked the entire night and completed her little house by dawn. She was delighted, but there was one flaw: there was no back door or side entrance. She ran to the study house to complain to her husband and ask him to take the builder to court. Reb Pesach quietened her anger. 'If the man built the cottage without a back door, it was probably not his own idea. It must have been decreed in heaven that Pesach

Radowieczer and his family should live in a house without a back door.'

Eventually Reb Pesach passed away peacefully. Later, the Nazis invaded Poland and darkness took over Europe. Radawiec was occupied and when the ghetto was liquidated Reb Pesach's family was sent to their deaths. Two of the grandchildren managed to escape deportation and hid in the cottage with no back door. They made a hiding place under the floor and covered the entrance with a large crate. The Germans had placed guards in front of Jewish homes to prevent looting while all valuables were crated and shipped to the fatherland. But the local Polish residents out-manoeuvred the guards by breaking in through the back doors. Often the guards turned a blind eye in return for the Poles handing over Jews who had managed to hide from them.

From their hiding place the two youngsters could hear Poles breaking into the builder's house by his back door. They heard the pleading voices of the family, begging not to be turned over to the Nazis – but to no avail. Moments after they were dragged away and the lads heard shots being fired, then – silence. The looters made for Reb Pesach's cottage, but found there was no back door, so they decided to move on to the next house.

During the night, the youngsters crept out of their hiding place and ran into the forest where they were given food and refuge by a friendly shepherd. They then made their way to a neighbouring town where able-bodied Jews were being made to work in a German factory. The two young men were sent to Majdaneck and then Auschwitz, where they were finally released by the advancing Allies.

They survived to recount this amazing story of how their lives had been saved by the fact that their grandparents' cottage had been constructed with no back door!

The Mysterious Generals

The Rabbi of Belz and his brother were on a visit to Poland when the Germans invaded the country. Both were smuggled out of the Warsaw Ghetto in May 1943. The Hungarian officer who organized the rescue was extremely well paid, and he devised a cunning but dangerous plan. He would pretend that he had been ordered to take back to Hungary two prominent Russian generals who had been captured on the Eastern front. The two generals were of course none other than the two rabbis. The officer had bribed contacts at various border checkpoints both in Poland and Hungary. He checked that all the forged documents were in perfect order. Everything had gone so smoothly that at one stop he dared to leave his two illustrious passengers alone in a car-park while he entered an inn to quench his thirst. When he returned, he could not find his car. After a frantic search he discovered that the car was precisely where he had left it – but it was shrouded in a heavy mist as if to conceal it from view. The officer was superstitious and feared that some unnatural force was somehow at work. He crossed himself as he said a silent prayer.

At the first major checkpoint in Hungary, the guard carefully examined the documents and compared the faces of the two passengers with the photos in their passports; then he checked their names against a list he had. 'Sorry I can't let you pass. I have no orders to expect the arrival of two captured generals,' he said.

The Hungarian officer assumed his most commanding tone. 'Check with your superior,' he demanded. The superior confirmed the soldier's statement.

The lad asked the two men in the back seat of the car: 'Where are your uniforms?'

Before they could reply the Hungarian officer barked: 'They are under strict orders to speak to no one except at headquarters.'

At that moment – out of the mist – there suddenly appeared three Hungarian high-ranking military officers mounted on horseback. They ordered the guard to let the captured generals through. The guard hurriedly obeyed and the car crossed the border on its way to freedom. The Hungarian officer was bewildered.

'I thought I knew all the generals in the Hungarian army – but I didn't recognize the three who came to our rescue,' he said.

'I did' quietly responded the Rabbi of Belz, with a smile on his lips. 'They were our father, our grandfather and our great grandfather . . . of blessed memory!'

A Good Samaritan

'My students, the time has come to abandon this house of worship and to escape wherever your paths will take you for the Communist authorities have ordered the closure of our synagogue. Go my sons . . . and may God go with you.'

Dovid was stunned. Orphaned at the age of four, cushioned ever since in the home of the rabbi and his wife, Dovid – now seventeen – was wholly unprepared to face the harsh world beyond the Russian study house.

'Go to Kiev', the rabbi had said, 'There you will find fellow Jews ready to help.'

At the railway station Dovid faced the booking office in sheer despair. How could he pay the fare when he hadn't even a kopek with which to bless himself? As the train was about to leave the platform he accidentally knocked down a peasant woman who almost fell under the train. She cursed him. A surge of humanity pressed forward, carrying him with them and he found himself on the train on his way to Kiev without ticket, without food, without anything. Soon the inspector entered their compartment. Panic stricken, Dovid turned to the same woman and appealed to her. She seemed unmoved, but then she took her own ticket and asked everyone around her: 'I don't see too well. Please, does my ticket take me to Kiev?' Then she surreptitiously thrust her ticket into Dovid's hand. To the inspector she enacted a great pretence of having mislaid it. She appealed to each and every person in the carriage, all of whom vouched for the fact that they had seen her ticket.

The inspector moved on. The woman winked at Dovid and crossed herself.

That stranger – a peasant woman he had almost killed – had most likely saved his life, for at that time a young religious Jew travelling across Russia in a train without a paid ticket would be bound to end up in Siberia for 20 or 30 years and would be unlikely to survive.

Dovid silently thanked God for sending him that good Samaritan who took pity on a penniless Jew.

The Saving Star

Michael Schwarz arrived in Auschwitz–Birkenau in August 1944 with one of the last transports from the Lodz Ghetto in Poland. Before he realized what was happening he was separated from his family and was led away in the opposite direction with a group of young men. The men were made to march beneath a barrage of leather truncheons, near the edges of a flaming pit where people were tossed alive.

A few hours later, his hair shaven, his body stinging from disinfectants, wearing a striped oversized uniform and a pair of skimpy broken clogs, Michael, along with hundreds of young men, was led off to a barracks. There he found a cousin from whom he had been separated earlier at the platform. That night in the barracks the cousins promise each other never to part again.

One day rumours spread that the impending selection was of particular importance, for those selected would be transferred out of Auschwitz to work at another camp. Michael was especially anxious to pass the selection for he had realized that Auschwitz would eventually devour everybody.

Dr Mengele himself was supervising the selection. He was using what was known among the Auschwitz old-timers as the 'washboard' criterion. Each inmate was ordered to lift his hands high above his head as he approached Mengele. If his rib cage protruded and each vertebra was clearly visible, Mengele would smile and motion with his snow-white glove to the left.

The moment came. Michael and his cousin stood in front of Mengele whose clean, shaven face glittered in the sun and whose eyes shone. The angel of death was in his moment of bliss. Michael's turn came and Mengele's finger pointed: 'Right!' Then Michael heard Mengele's death sentence on his cousin: 'Left!'

Michael stood before a table where three people sat dressed in white coats. One was holding a stamp pad, one a huge rubber stamp, and the third a pen and a white sheet of paper. Michael moved on to a group of young men wearing only a huge ink star on their foreheads. Michael realized that his star was the passport that would take him out of the camp and that his cousin in the other group just a few feet away would be sent to the chimneys.

In the commotion of the selection Michael decided to act. He walked briskly over to his cousin, spat on the lad's forehead, pressed his own forehead against his cousin's, took him by the hand, and led him to the group marked with stars. In the middle of his cousin's forehead was the imprint of the lucky star, the passport that led them out of the Auschwitz hell.

From Auschwitz Michael and his cousin were transported to six other concentration camps until they ended up in the Hermann Goering works in private companies engaged in the war industry.

On a May day in 1945 a tank entered a camp. On it was painted a huge white star and inside the tank sat a black-faced soldier wearing a steel helmet. After six years in the Nazi slave kingdom, Michael and his cousin were once again free men.

A Trick of Fate

Rabbi Moshe Kleinmann, his wife and twin sons had been arrested by the Nazis and immediately sent to the death camp where they were separated. Later he was told that his wife had been exterminated in the gas chamber and his twin sons had been handed over to the infamous Dr Mengele for experimentation.

The rabbi almost lost his faith in the Almighty. Being a strong man, still in his early forties, he was made to join the able-bodied inmates given to do the hardest labour. His fellow prisoners looked up to him for spiritual guidance and comfort and this partially restored his trust and faith. He managed to survive the hardship, the starvation diet and the beatings and was finally released when the Allies liberated the camp. After convalescing to restore his strength, Rabbi Kleinmann decided to move to Italy where he had friends. Deciding to break with the past he changed his name to Emmanuel Bosco and settled in the town of Pisa where before long he was invited to become the rabbi of the local Jewish congregation.

People urged him to remarry but he would not hear of it. The memory of his dear wife and beloved sons was too painful even though he attempted to push the wounds deep into the recesses of his subconscious.

Among his congregation was a dear busybody who was determined to act as matchmaker and find him a suitable bride, but she met with a blank wall of resistance. She decided to enlist the help of a friend in a nearby village who she knew had been a survivor from the extermination camps. He had since rebuilt his life and was now happily married with three lovely children. She thought he might prove a good example to Rabbi Bosco and she begged him to come to meet the good soul. He explained that he did not have the time but would gladly write a letter for her to give to the rabbi in which he urged him to prove to the Nazis that he had beaten them by creating a happy life and fathering a new family to perpetuate the line of his illustrious ancestors.

The good lady took the letter to Rabbi Bosco and insisted that he read it. He looked first at the signature and his face turned pale. With a sudden gasp for breath, he fainted. He had recognised the name and handwriting of one of his twin sons both of whom had escaped the grim reaper and survived vicious experiments performed on them by Dr Mengele, and by coincidence or fate or miraculous design, were now living with their respective families in a village only a few miles from their father in Pisa.

Flesh and Blood

Even before the last war, Jews in Poland, Russia and other countries in Eastern Europe were often subjected to pogroms, to Jew baitings and persecution. Many scrimped and saved in order to send their children to America – 'the land of hope and freedom'. Mr and Mrs Goldschmidt had eventually put by enough money for only one passage, and with tearful hearts they chose the oldest of their eight children and booked her passage to Baltimore in the States where her Aunt Manya was ready to welcome her with open arms.

Through the years the girl – Henya – received the occasional letter from home, letters which soon became wet with her tears and which she read and re-read until she knew them by heart. She had always been expecting her sisters and brothers to follow her at intervals when her parents would have saved enough to afford the small fortune for the fare, but Henya's hopes did not materialize. Then came the war: Hitler's armies invaded Poland and the letters ceased to arrive. Finally the dreaded news reached Henya that her home town had been denuded of its Jews and her entire family had perished in the concentration camps. Henya was devastated and it took a long time for her to recover from the shock.

During the time she hardly ever left the house, but when she eventually began to rebuild her life she met and fell in love with a charming young man of her own age called Daniel and they married. They were both sublimely happy, but this rapture was marred by the fact that she was unable to conceive. Daniel suggested they should adopt a child. At first Henya could not bring herself even to consider the idea for she was obsessed with the desire to have children of her own flesh and blood to compensate in some way for the loss of her family.

Time is a great healer and the day came when Henya accepted the idea and the couple placed their names on the waiting list of an adoption agency.

One morning the agency rang to say that a girl was now available and would they care to meet her. Henya was expecting to see a newly-born babe, but to her disappointment the girl turned out to be 8 years of age, and although she was gentle, sweet-natured and indeed a lovely girl, Henya rejected the idea, preferring to wait until the agency could provide her with a being she could bring up from babyhood as her very own.

A whole year elapsed and Henya began to despair. She felt that perhaps she should not have been so hasty in rejecting the girl because of her age. She had, after all, been a very appealing child and Henya had even felt she was somehow special. She rang the agency and was told that the girl had not been adopted in all that time. 'I'd like to reconsider the possibility if I may,' said Henya.

'There is one snag' replied the agent, 'since you were here last year we discovered a little brother of Miriam's languishing in an orphanage. They brought him here and now the two are inseparable. I feel it would be cruel to tear them apart. Won't you consider taking them both?'

At first Henya was reluctant, but after talking it over with Daniel, she relented and the two children duly arrived at their home on a probationary period while the necessary paperwork could be dealt with. The little boy, Moishe, was reticent and shy, but Miriam took to their new possible parents in a very loving manner and immediately won the hearts of both adults. On entering the dining room she was suddenly startled by a photograph on the piano of a middle-aged woman with a tender smile. She gasped and demanded 'Why have you got a photo of my grandmother on your piano? My Bubbe . . . why is the picture of my Bubbe on your piano?'

Henya was taken aback and for the moment was unable to answer. Miriam rushed to her suitcase and took out a much thumbed photo of another woman exclaiming: 'Look . . . this is my Mummy! Why have you got her mother's photo in your house?'

Henya stared at the photo Miriam showed her and turned pale. She recognized her own sister who had been slaughtered by the Nazis. She clasped Miriam fiercely to her breast as the floodgates of memory opened wide. They both burst into uncontrollable sobs. When she was able to speak, she said to her husband: 'Daniel – do you realize we have adopted the children of my own sister? God has sent us my very own flesh and blood!'

A Hairy Hand

I met him at my children's holiday camp where he baked bread and delighted the youngsters with biscuits in the shape of different animals. His name was Mr Slucky – the baker – but the children preferred to call him Mr Lucky. As usual my antenna was up and I gleaned a remarkable story from him. Let me tell you in his own words as far as I can remember them.

'I had a little sister who was the most beautiful person on earth. I loved her more than life itself. There was nothing I would not do for her. When the Germans occupied our town in Poland they rounded up all the young girls to take them as "comfort women" for the soldiers before offering them as fuel to the gas ovens. We hid her successfully for a while but one day on returning to the ghetto we found the door to our room had been broken and everything had been looted. My sister was gone. The Gestapo had taken her. I ran like a madman to the Gestapo headquarters and confronted a young soldier at the desk.

'"What's your wish, Jews, to be shot now? If you're in such a hurry I'll happily accommodate you," he said.

'"You took my sister," I shouted. "I want her back."

'"Who's your sister?"

'"The beautiful young girl you just brought in."

'A Gestapo officer came in from the next room and joined in the conversation. He burst out laughing. "I tell you what, Jew – I'll let your beautiful sister go on one condition – that right now you'll grow hair on the palm of your hand." Both men laughed till I thought they'd choke.

'I opened my hand – it was covered in black hair. The Gestapo officer screamed hysterically, "You Jewish Satan – take your sister and run before I machine-gun the two of you."

'We raced home faster than an Olympic champion, I'm sure. We stopped just long enough for my parents to see that my sister was safe, then we fled to the forest. You see, as a boy I used to work in a factory and my hand got caught in a machine. It was terribly mangled, but the surgeon somehow managed to save it. He took skin from a hairy part of my body to graft on to my palm and in my late teens hair began to grow on it.'

Mr 'Lucky' opened his hand – and there I clearly saw a thick growth of black hair!

A Miraculous Leap

According to Jewish tradition when you are in dire need, the merits earned by your predecessors on this earth will be chalked up in your favour.

During the Nazi Holocaust, occupants of Auschwitz were subjected to 'selections' at which many of the prisoners were sent to the gas chambers. On one particular day the men selected were ordered to march several miles to a field where they were made to dig a deep trench 10 ft wide. They worked through that night, the next day and the night that followed, without food or drink. Lime was then thrown into the pit and the prisoners were told to stand naked by the edge of the deep hole.

The commandant then announced 'I am not unmerciful . . . and I am prepared to grant a release to all those among you who can manage a simple task. I want you to leap over the hole. Those who succeed may walk away free. Those who do not, will fall into the pit and will be covered by earth to be thrown over them by the guards.' Among the men awaiting certain death in this sadistic jest was the learned Rabbi of Lodz. Now, almost alone in the world of the near-dead, his best friend and opponent in the camp was a confirmed atheist who delighted in trying to prove the non-existence of the Almighty. The atheist placed his threadbare shirt round the shoulder of the rabbi when the order came to jump and one by one the men fell into the hole.

To the amazement of the commandant the rabbi and his

arch-opponent successfully leapt over the 10 ft-wide pit to land safely on the other side. The atheist, agog with wonder, asked: 'Rabbi, how did you manage it?'

'I knew my ancestors were rooting on my behalf and I merely hoped that their prayers would help to weight the scales in my favour. As I jumped I clung to the merit of my ancestors. But tell me, my friend, what did you cling to?'

'I? I clung to the shirt on your back!' replied the atheist.

Have Faith – He Is Alive

My friend Hannah survived years of incarceration in Auschwitz concentration camp. Her parents were less fortunate and met their demise in the gas chambers, but an aunt and uncle had seen the writing on the wall early enough and had managed to leave Hungary before the Nazi invasion. They found refuge in Switzerland. Her step-brother had escaped in time to join Tito's partisans in Yugoslavia. Hannah and he had been very attached and as communication was not possible she did not know if he were still alive, but an inner voice whispered 'have faith . . . he is'.

During the Hungarian revolution Hannah managed to flee the country and made her way to Switzerland.

Exhausted and deeply affected by the fact that her parents had succumbed to the Nazi extermination and feeling somehow guilty that she should have been spared, Hannah fell into a state of depression and feared to leave her uncle's apartment. For several months she remained in a prison of her own creating and her aunt began to fear for her sanity.

One morning – for no apparent reason – Hannah announced that she was going for a walk. Her aunt was astonished but pleased.

'Wait for me, Hannah . . . I'll go with you.'

'Please, Auntie, I'm not a little girl that I need you to hold my hand. I know I've been behaving strangely and you've been an angel to put up with my fears, but this morning I'm feeling more like my old self – and I don't know why – I have an urgent need to go out right now.'

Hannah set off and soon found herself in the main square and – walking dazed and uncertain – she bumped into a man who turned and politely apologized. The two took one look at each other – and both burst into tears.

The young man was none other than her step-brother.

A Change of Heart

The year was 1940 – soon after France had been overrun by the Nazi invaders. In a synagogue in Lyons a small group of Jews had gathered, preparing to usher in the sabbath. As the service drew to an end, those present chanted the traditional melody 'Come my Beloved' – a hymn that gives tidings of redemption. At the conclusion of this prayer it is customary in many synagogues for the entire congregation to turn round and face the entrance at the back of the room. As they turned – directly facing them – was a group of Nazi sympathizers, all masked, their hand grenades at the ready as they prepared for a massacre. They certainly had not expected the Jews to turn and face them directly. They had planned to sneak in behind them and hurl their grenades at the men, women and children, while rapidly making their escape; but the French Jews just stood there – staring, transfixed – and the Nazi followers had a sudden change of heart. Still holding their deadly grenades, they backed out of the synagogue.

The rabbi addressed the congregation, a slight tremor audible in his voice: 'Fellow Jews, we are safe because at the moment of gravest danger we turned to face the door to welcome the sabbath, the bride of Israel. The men of evil have gone, but the bride remains. Let us greet her.'

Mamma

On one of my many trips to Israel, I happened to arrive at the time of the annual Holocaust Survivors' Convention. Outside Ben Gurion Airport I joined several people in a cherut – one of those private taxis that transport five passengers for little more than the bus fare. It was full and before long the occupants began to tell each other why they had come: in search of loved ones from whom they had been separated in the Nazi death camps . . . and for whom the doubtful hope still remained that perhaps – just perhaps – they might also have survived and were drawn to Israel for this heartbreaking convention.

One lady had remained silent while the others spoke. Everyone turned to look at her as she shyly debated within herself whether or not to tell her story. A silent voice argued that she was only wasting her time yet again. This was not the first time she had joined the hundreds of broken lives desperately praying to find a husband, a child, a sister or brother who might also chance to be present – and who knows – who knows?

The other occupants of the cherut were growing impatient as the lady seemed to be arguing with her conscience. Her silence seemed to hide a heartrending scream, as though it were telling her that to voice her suffering would only be tempting providence and stifling that spark of hope which still flickered in her heart. 'You know you have travelled here five times already and each time you have left more desperate than before. Isn't it time you accepted the inevitable and realized once and for all that you will never find your child?' Finally the floodgates burst and Luba spoke up.

In the Warsaw Ghetto the Nazis had gathered all the Jews on to the street where they were made to stand the entire night in the blinding rain and freezing air. At dawn the selection had begun. 'You . . . to the right! You . . . to the left!' But which side meant immediate despatch and which meant permission to linger on as slave labourers in the extermination camps – who could know?

Luba Czernak – for that was her name – had been separated from her little 9-year-old son Modche and sent to the right. She, her husband Aaron and their daughters were pushed to the left. Aaron rushed forward to grab their little Modche, and was shot on the spot by the commanding officer. Only Luba and the boy survived – but where had they taken her rosy-cheeked, chubby little treasure? Will she ever see him again?

Within three months, her remaining children had died of starvation. It was then that Luba made a pact with the Almighty. She forced herself to believe that He had taken the rest of her family in order to prevent any further suffering. She would never lose faith in God – but in return she asked that He would spare her Modche. When the Americans liberated the camp she began a frantic search through the Red Cross files – all to no avail. Modche had vanished with the thousands of others whose fate remained unknown.

Now, she had come yet again to the Holocaust Reunion in a last attempt to see if he were alive and might also have come. In the event that were to be the case – and to help him to recognize her, she had decided to don a T-shirt which she now held up for the others to see. On it she had embroidered the words:

I AM LUBA CZERNAK FROM LODZ

LOOKING FOR MY SON MODCHE ISROEL

BORN IN LODZ ON THE 14TH OF DECEMBER 1931.

As she finished reading the words aloud the cab driver suddenly slammed on his brakes, throwing the occupants to the floor. His eyes bulged, his mouth opened wide and a primal scream rent the air:

'MAMMA!'

Forbidden to Fast

Kalmann Mann and his 16-year-old son Yitzhak were arrested by the Germans who had occupied Budapest in Hungary and sent to a labour camp to be worked to death by the Nazis. After a few months the two managed to escape and make their way back to Budapest. There Yitzhak was able to infiltrate the Hungarian Fascist youth movement known as the Green Shirts. He lived in a youth camp where he was able to gather information about planned actions against the Jews and to filter this back to the Zionist leaders in the capital.

One day, as Yitzhak was lining up for his meal, the young Hungarian officer who was handing out the food whispered to him in Yiddish, 'They suspect you! Run!' Yitzhak was astonished. This jolly young man so full of patriotic Fascist jokes and songs and who looked like a typical Hungarian peasant, was after all a Jew, like himself! Yitzhak took the hint and discreetly slipped out of the camp.

Soon after he and his father were again rounded up in the street together with other Jews and again taken to a labour camp. There they were made to stand with the other inmates while a German officer addressed them through a loud-hailer. 'You are now under the direct command of the Todt Organization, and as such, you are soldiers of the Third Reich. You are fortunate people who will benefit from the generosity of the German Fatherland.'

34

The men who were hearing this 'sweet' approach for the first time filled their minds with hope – but Kalmann Mann, Yitzhak's father, was not taken in by the officer's declaration. He had heard it all before! That clean-shaven, smartly dressed, smooth-tongued Nazi could not fool him! He knew from bitter experience what it meant for a Jew to be a 'soldier' in the Jewish labour battalion. It meant digging ditches, building roads and burying butchered Jews. The 'honour' of being a German soldier also meant being a living mine detector! Kalmann was one among 250 Jews who were chosen to cross a Russian minefield. First they were given a pep talk, stressing how honoured they should feel at being selected to take part in Germany's great war against Communism. After the talk they were ordered to march into the minefield. Of the 250 men only 50 returned. Kalmann Mann had been among those lucky ones.

The Russians launched a huge offensive and the Germans were forced to beat a hasty retreat. The Jewish labour battalion was then made to demolish all communications and dwellings, railroad tracks and bridges. The Nazis were following a scorched-earth policy and the Jews were forced to be perpetrators.

On the eve of Yom Kippur, the commander gave his customary long speech: 'I know that tomorrow is one of your holiest days and you are commanded to fast. I must remind you that soldiers at war are strictly forbidden to fast. All those who attempt to do so will be executed by firing squad. I will tolerate no violations! Is that understood?'

On that Day of Atonement the Jews worked as usual. It rained heavily and the ground rapidly became a muddy swamp. When food was given them, with one accord the men emptied the coffee into the pools of rainwater and hid the stale bread beneath their soaking jackets.

When night came, they fell exhausted at the Mount of Bornemissza and calculated when it was time to break their fast. At that moment the German commander ordered them all to line up for roll-call. The men feared the worst. Fathers embraced their sons and they bade each other farewell. The officer embarked on another of his famous speeches. His voice was sweet and he smiled benevolently.

'I know that you disobeyed my instructions not to fast today, but I am a generous man and I am not going to punish you with execution as you deserve under the law. Instead, you are going to climb that mountain ahead and slide down on your stomachs. Those among you who wish to repent may here and now admit that they were wrong to disobey my orders and they will find me magnanimous in my reaction. Raise your hands all those who wish to do so and to avail themselves of my good heartedness.'

In the utter silence that followed, not a single hand went up. So, exhausted, soaked to the skin, their stomachs starving, the Jews began to climb the mountain and to slide down on their stomachs. When they reached the bottom, they were ordered to line up again. They were asked if any of them now wanted to repent – but again not a single voice responded. Ten times they were ordered to repeat that humiliating and inhuman exercise and each time they did so with greater determination and newly found strength.

At midnight when the rains abated, they were ordered to stop and were given food and drink. They lit small fires, attempting to dry out their clothes and to warm their freezing bodies. Their faces shone with a strange glow of pride and defiance. A young German soldier walked up to the group where Kalmann and his son Yitzhak were seated, and said:

'I don't know who will win this war – but of one thing I

am certain. People like you – a nation like yours – will never be defeated. Never!'

This story was related by Yitzhak himself – now a success-ful rabbi and charismatic speaker.

The Hiding Place

' "Daddy, you haven't tucked me in."

'What a weight of reproach there can be in the voice of a child.

' "Yes, dear, I'm coming."

'The doctor with whom I was conversing excused himself. We both understood that being tucked in was of much greater importance than any economic problems we might be discussing. He went upstairs and I heard the sounds of a minute's romping, the chatter of two children's voices, and then the footsteps of the doctor as he returned down the stairs. We went on with our conversation, but my mind was no longer on the subject. The doctor and his wife were Jews, the Gestapo might arrive at any moment to snatch those children from their beds, and drag them off to some camp for a sudden or lingering death. Would the father be taken away from his family and the mother mourn for her children in far away Poland?

' "Daddy, did you know that you hadn't tucked me in?" '

That was Corrie Ten Boom talking to me in Haarlem in Holland where I was acting in a film of her life. If the name is not familiar – engrave it on your minds as it is already in the hearts of so many of her fellow countrymen whose lives she saved from the Nazis during the war.

Papa Ten Boom was a gentle 82-year-old Dutch clockmaker in Haarlem, living uneventfully with his two middle-aged daughters when the German invasion of Holland cut across their lives like cheese-wire.

A deeply religious Christian, Papa Ten Boom had brought up his four children in a thorough grounding of the Hebrew Bible, which he loved – and through that Book, the Jews whom he called 'the apple of God's eye'.

His son Willem had taken holy orders in the Dutch Reform Church, but his health had forced him to retire. Willem shared his father's love for 'the people of the Book'. Although missionary by inclination, he did not try to change people, just to serve them. He scrimped and saved enough money to build a home for elderly Jews in Hilversum, and during Hitler's early anti-Semitic measures, a deluge of young German Jews who had escaped over the border descended on his house. Willem turned no one from his door and he and his family gave up their own living quarters to sleep in a corridor.

After the German armies invaded Holland, unknown to his father and sisters, Willem joined a resistance group and organized hide-outs for countless Jews for whom he obtained false documents and ration books.

When Corrie and Betsie discovered this, they insisted on turning their own home into a 'hiding place'. A false brick wall was built in Corrie's bedroom, behind which the refugees hid whenever strangers or German soldiers called, and however small the daily rations were, no one was allowed to go hungry.

Eventually, they were betrayed by a Dutch collaborator. The SS brutally beat up the sisters and arrested the entire family, but they never discovered the hiding place, and after three days and nights of hunger, total darkness and terror, the refugees escaped.

The Ten Booms were interrogated for weeks in Scheveningen prison, where Corrie was kept in solitary confinement. Her father had fallen ill in his cell and had been taken to a hospital where no bed was available. He died in a corridor, with no clue to his identity and was buried in the paupers' cemetery.

From Scheveningen the two sisters were moved to a camp in Vught and later deported to that hell of hells known as Ravensbruck. Betsie finally succumbed, leaving Corrie to survive the starvation and the unbelievable terror.

She was finally released after 18 months on condition she signed a form stating that she had never been ill in the camp, had never had an accident and that her treatment had been good. Later she learned that her release had been the result of a 'clerical error'. One week after, all women of her age had been taken to the gas chambers.

In her late eighties, still vigorous and firm, Corrie continued to travel the world bringing her message of faith and love, and the truth she learned in Ravensbruck where 96,000 women died: the truth that God can turn adversity into a means to do good, and that man's love for man must extend to his bitterest enemy.

The Bag-Lady

The Kotel in Jerusalem – commonly known as the Wailing Wall – is like a meeting place of the United Nations. People come from the four corners of the world to pay their respects or to pray. The first time I visited it with my wife, we noticed a poorly dressed woman carrying her possessions in two plastic bags. We had seen her before in the town, holding out her hand to passers-by and we understood that she was homeless, and completely dependent on the goodwill of others. Apparently she was one of those Holocaust survivors who had bottled up the memory of the trauma they had undergone at the hands of the Germans, who would not talk about it to their relatives or to others, but who later in life suffered dreadful nightmares in which they relived their experiences. They were known to cry out in terror during the night, believing they were still locked within those ghastly years which they had attempted to bury in their subconscious minds.

My wife had given her some money and in return received a lovely, friendly smile that immediately warmed her to us. The woman approached the wall, placed her bags gently on the ground and covered her eyes with her hands in prayer. When she had finished, she rummaged through one of the bags and took out a stub of a pencil. Then she ripped off a piece of paper and began to write. She folded the paper very neatly and wedged it into a small crevice between the stones of the wall. After that she turned and shuffled away.

The paper fell on to the ground. My wife bent down to pick it up and put it back. As she held it in her hand and lifted it towards the stones, the paper unfolded. Tina looked at it and I could see a tear welling up in her eye. She showed me the paper and the words on it moved me too. That poor, homeless woman who perhaps owned nothing but the contents of those two plastic bags had scribbled on the paper in ill-formed childish writing the simple words: 'God – I love You.' I realized that although she may have had little in the way of material possessions, she was nevertheless completely content in her relationship with the Almighty. Tina and I looked at each other and we both had moist eyes. Tina wedged the folded paper tightly into the crevice and we walked away in silence.

Natan the Soldier

Natan Kotowski – a Polish Jew – was a death-camp survivor. The story he told me was most unusual. As a child he had lived with his parents in a rural town not far from the Russian border. He encountered a good deal of anti-Semitism at school. His neighbours, however, were friendly and Natan used to enjoy playing football with their children in the street and the nearby park. When the Germans invaded his hometown, those friendly neighbours suddenly turned on the family and denounced them to the Nazis who arrested his parents and older brother. However, prompted by his mother, Natan had hidden among the straw in the loft of their barn and after the soldiers left, he made his way across the border at night, avoiding detection by the guards.

He thought he would be safe in Russia where he had an uncle whom he was sure would give him succour. However, on the way to his uncle's farm he was caught by Russian police who immediately arrested him as he had no papers or documents to prove his identity. Thrown into jail he languished there for several weeks, sharing a cell with a pimp and a pickpocket who deprived him of his wallet and the little money he still had. He was then dragged before someone he took to be a magistrate who questioned him closely, then offered him the choice of a lengthy prison sentence or to join the Red Army immediately. Wisely, Natan chose the latter. He was then whisked off in a caged-van to a military depot where he was handed an ill-fitting uniform and given an upper bunk in an overcrowded wooden hut. His fellow-conscripts began by glowering at him in an unfriendly manner, then ignored him completely.

Night was falling fast and Natan followed the lead of most of the men by neatly folding his garments at the end of his bed and climbing under a coarse blanket which smelt as though it had never seen soap and water – which it probably hadn't! All were awakened in the early morning by a severe-sounding sergeant who ordered the men to get dressed and assemble in the square outside. Natan found that during the night his good sturdy boots had been exchanged for an old dilapidated pair several sizes too small for his feet, and his new army shirt was missing. He protested to his fellow recruits whose only response was to beat him and assail his ears with a tirade of threats and obscenities. On the parade ground the sergeant began to lecture them about what they could expect from him if they did not obey his every command and, stopping before Natan who was standing stiffly to attention in his vest and trousers minus braces, said:

'Ah! A smart Alec who flogged his shirt and braces for a few roubles! Fine beginning, my son . . . you'll go far . . . all the way to the dog house! What's your name?'

'Natan Kotowski, sgt.'

'Natan? Sounds biblical. Are you one of them?'

'Sorry sgt. I'm not sure who you mean.'

'Jews, you fool. Are you a Jew?'

'Afraid so, sgt.' The sergeant turned to the rest of the men and called out sarcastically: 'What d'you know?! We have a Polish Yid in our midst! Suits me fine! We need a strong latrine cleaner!'

He turned to a soldier standing by him. 'Corporal . . . assign this Yid to latrine duty. And keep a sharp eye on him to make sure he does a thorough job. I don't allow slackers in my platoon. Is that clear . . . Comrade Yid?! I know you don't eat pork but the pigs'll have no objection to making short shrift of you!'

A quiet sniggering could be heard among the men, soon made to cease by a thunderous command from the sergeant.

From that moment every dirty task was immediately assigned to Natan. He was made to empty the officers' slops, to clean and polish the sergeant's boots whether they needed it or not, to carry the heavy buckets of potatoes to the 'grub house' and to scrub each one until it positively shone!

After the briefest period of training, Natan was despatched with the rest of the platoon directly to the front line. Before long few of them remained alive, sent to their maker under the withering fire of a German army better equipped, rigorously trained and highly disciplined. The men had dug a long trench where they took shelter, firing over the top whenever there was a lull in the bombardment.

After a few days an amazing thing happened: the Germans facing them had run out of ammunition and word reached their commanding officer that the Russians had launched a counter-attack behind their lines and were advancing in a pincer movement, entirely circling the Germans, who were not trapped. Faced with the possibility of his men being completely wiped out, the commanding officer decided to surrender. The white flag was displayed and the officer yelled across the short area of no man's land, requesting to parley with his opposite number if he would send someone across to accept the surrender. Knowing that the ground between the two forces was heavily mined, the Russian sergeant could easily have insisted that the German cross over to him, but he saw this as an opportunity to get rid of the 'Jew-boy', so he ordered Natan to make his way over to the opposite trench. Natan had no alternative but to obey.

Rifle in hand, he climbed out of the trench, called out in

Hebrew 'Shema Yisrael, Adonai Elohenu, Adonai Echad' (The Lord our God, the Lord is One) and ran across the pot-holed ground to the German line in a zig-zag fashion and dropped into their dug-out. The men who hoped and expected this Russian soldier would be blown to kingdom come could hardly believe their eyes and, despite themselves, with one accord they applauded his dexterity in avoiding the mines. Although they had chosen to surrender, they were unwilling to follow him back across the perilous ground, so Natan took it upon himself to order them to lay down their weapons, raise their hands above their heads and march in the opposite direction toward the advancing Russians.

Natan told me that after this episode, his sergeant changed his attitude towards him and even recommended him for promotion for his bravery.

Later, Natan was captured by the Germans and when they realized he was a Jew, he was examined by their medical officer who pronounced him fit and healthy. The Germans had received orders to shoot weak, elderly or Jewish women and children but to send able-bodied men to a concentration camp where they could be put to heavy work as long as there was life left in them. This way, Natan found himself among hundreds of his fellow Jews, working day and night for their Nazi masters. After a few months of starvation rations he fell ill with a high fever and in spite of his weakness, was made to dig a trench beyond the camp together with other sick inmates, then to stand naked at the edge as each was shot in the back of the neck. He timed the lapse between each shot and when his turn came, he dropped into the ditch a second before the shot, and was soon covered in a sea of bodies of the other unfortunate souls.

After two long days spent beneath the rotting flesh, he

managed to crawl out of the ditch at night time and to escape into the nearby forest where he survived on roots and leaves until the Germans were ordered to retreat before the advancing Russians, leaving the remaining Jews in the camp to fend for themselves.

When it was safe to emerge, he made his way to Prague where a Jewish family took care of him. When I met him there he was earning a reasonable living as a taxi driver and saving to pay his fare to the States. He had scars on his face and body from the many beatings he had received at the hands of the Germans. The muscles of his left arm were damaged where he had been hit with a spade by a sadistic guard but his disposition was cheerful and optimistic. His motto in life was 'whatever happens is for the best'. I offered to pay the balance he still needed for the air fare, but he was too proud to accept.

I salute you, Natan Kotowski, and I pray that you will reach the States in good health. I am grateful to you for telling me your story.

The One-Legged Man

In Israel I met a man with a wooden leg, bravely coping with his handicap, even managing to joke about it. Someone had told him of my desire to collect Holocaust stories – particularly those that showed how people had overcome their nightmare experience at the hands of the Nazis. Noah was very willing to talk and he plunged straight into a moving narrative.

'I know you are going to question me about my false leg, so I'll save you the trouble by answering you before you do so. It's a long story, but I'll make it brief. I'm a survivor of not one but four different death camps. I made friends with a man from my home town in Poland who happened to be a Gypsy violinist as well as an ex-circus man. He was arrested by the Germans while performing at a Jewish wedding, and no matter how much he insisted that he was not a Jew his captors protested that as he was caught at a Jewish wedding – as far as they were concerned – he was a Jew! His own people were equally persecuted by the Germans, so he decided he might just as easily go up the gas chimneys as a Jew.

'I loved that man. He stifled his empty stomach pains with a delightful sense of humour and could manage to draw a smile even from the saddest among us. We pricked our thumbs and linked our blood as a token of brotherhood and we swore that if we survived the incarceration, we'd remain like David and Jonathan for the rest of our lives. Fate decided otherwise and after the war we lost track of

48

each other – but I was certain in my heart that Pyotr was alive and that I would find him one day. I put out feelers all over the globe and one day I received news that after liberation he had linked up with a group of other survivors making their way to Israel. There he joined a kibbutz, farming in the desert. So that's where I decided to go to find him.'

'And did you?' I asked.

Noah's eyes clouded over and he was silent for a long moment.

'Unfortunately not. He died of a heart attack three weeks before I arrived in the kibbutz. You may imagine my grief. Pyotr was very popular, especially with the children. He came from a circus family as I told you and he formed a mini-troupe among the boys and girls and taught them all he knew. Apparently the group had become famous and were often invited to perform for foreign dignitaries and important visitors. I was in shock for several days when I heard that he had died – but then I decided to stay on at the kibbutz and to take over Pyotr's work in the fruit-juice factory. I felt that would somehow draw me closer to him in spirit even though his physical being had left this earth. The work entailed emptying mounds of fruit into the enormous grinding machine that produces the juice. It was not difficult although very tiring.

'One morning the motor jammed and I climbed on top of the pile of fruit to see what the problem was, when suddenly it started up again. I slipped and fell on to the apples. I could see the blades grinding away and getting closer and closer to me. I tried to climb out of the hopper but its smooth sloping sides had nothing to grab on to. I screamed for help, but no one could hear me. The next thing I knew, my foot was trapped in the jaws of the huge blades which continued to chop up my leg as though it were caramel. The pain was excruciating and just as I was losing consciousness I felt a strong pair of hands grasp me by the shoulders and drag me clear of the hopper. I couldn't see the man's face but I caught sight of his arm which had a number tattooed on it. It was 492603. That was Pyotr's number as a prisoner in the concentration camp. It was the number following mine which was 492602 and I recognized Pyotr's immediately. How could I ever forget it? My Gypsy friend whom I loved as a brother had returned from the beyond to save my life! An artificial leg was made for me and I stayed on in the kibbutz to continue Pyotr's work, as a tribute to his memory.

'I now manage the children's circus and arrange their performances. We renamed it "Pyotr's Children" and we have performed in capitals all over the world.

'Now you know my story – and you can spread it far and wide, for every time you tell it, I am sure Pyotr's spirit will smile up there and you'll make my ears buzz with pleasure. Don't forget that wonderful old Jewish phrase: "No man is truly dead as long as he is remembered!" '

Rulenka

I met her in Prague during the Friday evening service in the beautiful Spanish synagogue – an elderly, poorly dressed lady whose face showed traces of earlier beauty tempered by time and sorrow. My ears rather than my eyes first drew me to notice her, for she had a glorious singing voice which captured the attention of all the congregants. Her face was heavily lined and the skin tanned by the sun and wind, but her eyes were bright and young and seemed to smile as she spoke. We got into conversation and my antenna drew out her story.

Rulenka had been an opera singer trained and performed in Vienna until the fact that she was a Jew made it impossible for her to obtain employment and she managed to move to Prague hoping that the Czech people would be less welcoming to the Nazi occupiers, but it proved to be a classic case of 'from the frying pan . . .' Her time was spent moving from one hiding place to another. Finally she found an attic room in a poor quarter of the town where the land-lady made her feel she'd be safe. In a nearby cafe she made the acquaintance of a younger woman called Marta who told her: 'I am blonde and fair skinned, so I am taken for a typical Aryan and left in peace, but don't be fooled by my appearance . . . I am Jewish.'

Marta advised Rulenka to stay in her room during the day and never to wander far at night if she were tempted to go out. The local police and those sympathetic to the Germans were forever on the prowl, ferreting out hidden

Jews and denouncing them to the Germans. If Rulenka were to be caught, the likelihood of her ever being seen again was almost nil!

Rulenka took the hint and spent the daylight hours cooped up in her small attic with nothing but her memories for company. Whenever she entered the room a strange sensation assailed her. She was extremely sensitive to atmosphere and could always tell if a place had happy or tragic connections. At night her slumber was disturbed by a recurring nightmare. She dreamt that the cul-de-sac where she lived ended in a high wall dotted with red stains which resembled dried blood. In her dream she could see herself making toward the wall with fear in her heart as she could hear the sound of jack-boots following her, but the owners of those boots remained unseen – a fact that proved all the more menacing. The closer she came to the wall, the more it receded and she feared she would never reach it. The sound of marching steps was getting closer and closer until she wanted to scream with fear – but no sound emerged from her open lips.

Suddenly the iron cover to a street sewer mysteriously opened up before her. She climbed into the hole and drew the cover just in time to hear the regular stamping of the jackboots pass above and recede beyond. The smell in the sewer was nauseating and she could see excrement of rats mingled with the mud on the concrete floor beneath the metal ladder she was clinging to. She forced herself to descend and walk along the tunnel, without knowing where it would lead. She felt as though a myriad eyes were following her every step. The eyes of rats were everywhere around her. Suddenly a German voice called out, echoing down the tunnel. 'Here . . . here . . . she must be here!'

Rulenka would then awaken and her whole body was wet with the perspiration. She feared to go to sleep again in case the nightmare should return. One day she was tempted to tell Marta of her dream and the woman gazed at her in wonder.

'You must be extremely psychic,' Marta told her, 'that wall you describe is the one where Jews are made to stand facing it and the Germans shoot them in the back; and the red colour you see on the wall is spattered blood. I belong to a resistance group and my job is to take Jews who are hiding in attic rooms like the one where you live to the same sewer near the wall which you've described in your nightmare – and to guide them through the labyrinth of tunnels which lead to the edge of the city and pass them on to other members of the group who help them to escape into the woods and from there to disperse into the countryside.'

Eventually Marta warned Rulenka that it was no longer safe to remain in her attic room and offered to escort her through the same tunnels.

'I walked for miles in the countryside,' Rulenka told me, 'until I found a farmhouse where the owner and his wife were friendly and hid me from the Germans. I used to sleep in the hayloft where I could bury myself deep in the hay if the Nazis came in search of escaping Jews. Later when the Germans had been defeated and the Communists took over the country, it was safe to emerge from my hiding place – but without documents or papers to prove who I was my movements were severely restricted and I was not able to leave the country. I had to report to the police every few days and the members of this Spanish synagogue fed and housed me. Now I can earn my keep by singing at weddings and different functions. When I have saved enough I hope to buy a ticket to return to Vienna and study again under a wonderful opera singer who has now retired and teaches, and ... who knows ... if I am lucky, one day I might be able to resume my career.'

I took out my wallet and asked to be permitted the privilege of contributing towards her fare to Vienna, but she looked at me with such hurt in her eyes that I realized I had offended her with my suggestion – and she walked away from me in the driving rain with no protection for her hair. Her head was held high and she walked with pride and dignity. I am sure the day will come when I will recognize her face on a poster outside a Vienna Opera House and I will join the audience to find myself thrilled by the sound of this diva – as I was in the Spanish synagogue during that Friday night service in praise of the Almighty whose mysterious ways are wondrous to behold!

Mother and Daughter

Perhaps one of the most bizarre Holocaust stories I have encountered is the one concerning Jessica M—. She and her 13-year-old daughter Marianne were the only members of her entire family to remain alive during the decimation the Nazis perpetrated on the Jews. All seven of Jessica's other children, her husband, two brothers and one sister had been murdered by men of the 'pure Aryan race' and Jessica and Marianne had been transferred to the women's section at Ravensbruck concentration camp. Marianne was very mature for her age and Jessica had managed to pass her off as 16. This saved her from being 'selected' for the gas chamber – but it also meant that the girl was forced to do the work of a sturdy adult, which made life extremely tough for a 13-year-old.

Marianne fell ill and developed pneumonia. Her mother was in despair, knowing that if the camp commandant were to be informed, the child would immediately be liquidated. During the daily roll call she and a friend supported the sick child as they stood her up between them in the freezing compound. Immediately after, Marianne was put back on the hard bunk bed and both women gave up their flimsy blankets to add to Marianne's. Jessica had sacrificed her bread ration day after day to sustain her child, depriving herself to the point of near starvation.

A German officer paid an unexpected visit to their hut and noticed the condition of Marianne. He stared hard at her, then at her mother without saying a word, then left the hut. Jessica began to weep uncontrollably, anticipating that her precious child – the only remaining one of the entire brood – would now be taken from her to be added to the ashes of the countless others who had been feeding the fires of the gas chambers, when suddenly the officer returned carrying a cauldron of hot soup – not the wishy-washy potato-peel kind the inmates were normally given, but a nourishing soup with pieces of meat inside – something the women had not seen since they were first arrested. Silently he placed the cauldron on the bunk by Marianne, handed a ladle to Jessica and gestured to her to feed her daughter. He then placed his finger to his lips as if to indicate that no one should know – and left the hut again.

For the next week this exercise was repeated daily – always in silence. Marianne's high fever subsided and she even put on a little weight. One day when it was his turn to take the roll-call of prisoners, that same officer ordered Jessica and Marianne to stay behind after dismissing the rest of the women and he whispered to Jessica: 'I had a little girl who looked very like your daughter. I loved her dearly – but she died of pneumonia. Don't let the same happen to your child.' Then he dropped his voice even lower and muttered: 'My great grandfather was a Jew – but if you ever tell anyone . . . anyone . . . you understand, I'll shoot you both. Is that clear?'

Not long after that, the prisoners were assembled in the compound and the commandant ordered that same officer to be brought forward. A beaten, almost unrecognizable man was dragged before him by two rough guards. The commandant then addressed the women: 'It has come to my notice that this officer has been feeding one of your Jewish brats with extra rations. This is strictly forbidden and merits the punishment of death. I am going to make an example of this despicable cur who has disgraced the uniform, our beloved Führer and the honour of the victorious

German army. He has proved to be no better than all you Jewish scum and I invite you all to see how we punish our own when they disobey the Führer's orders.' He commanded the beaten officer to drop to his knees before him, drew his revolver and whipped the man across the face, first one cheek, then the other, then he pointed his weapon at the man's forehead and shot him directly between the eyes.

'He doesn't deserve to be buried. Leave his carcass in the centre of the compound for all to see, until it rots before their eyes!'

By the morning the body of the officer had mysteriously disappeared and the entire inmates were punished by having their meagre food rations withdrawn for three whole days. Jessica and several of the women managed secretly to bury the corpse which was never discovered.

Both mother and daughter survived the war and were liberated by the American troops who overran the camp. When peace finally came, Jessica made it her business to check through the Red Cross and records of the camp in order to find the name and the address of that officer's family, whom she visited in Berlin. She told the widow of his kind gesture which had saved the life of her daughter and she gave her the buttons of his army jacket which she had cut off and kept hidden against the day when she could offer them to the man's wife.

'I kissed these buttons every night as I said a prayer for his soul,' she told her. 'Your husband was a truly noble man and my daughter and I will never forget his compassion and generosity of spirit. He made us proud once again to be German – and I share with you the loss of that German officer who took pity on a Jewish girl in the midst of the hatred, cruelty and contempt of his fellow-officers. May his soul rest in peace.'

The officer's name has been added to the scroll of

'Righteous among the nations' in Israel, where it will be honoured for ever.

This story was told to me by Jessica herself when I met her at a survivors gathering in Israel. Jessica and Marianne are not their real names.

The Lord's Visit

In the town of Eisysky in Lithuania, many of the local population were happy to work for the Germans who employed them to round up the Jews and to search for any who avoided capture. The unfortunate men, women and children were taken in groups of 250 to the old Jewish cemetery in front of ditches which had been dug for a special purpose. There they were ordered to undress and stand naked by the edge of the open graves. One by one they were shot in the back of the head by Lithuanian guards in full view of delighted local people who had come to watch and applaud the slaughter. Among the victims was a well-liked teacher named Reb Michalowsky and his youngest son Zvi, aged 16. They held hands as Zvi counted the bullets and the intervals between one volley of fire and the next. He planned to follow a tactic already adopted by other victims – and he whispered it to his father. As the guns were being aimed, he dropped on to the grave a second before the bullets reached him. He was counting on his father doing the same thing but unfortunately their fingers slipped from each other's hands – and it was too late. But not for him. Bodies piled on top of him, covering him completely. He could feel the spurts of blood streaming from the victims over and around him and the death jerks of their dying limbs beneath him.

When the shooting had died down, he could hear the Lithuanians singing and drinking as they celebrated their great accomplishment. They were now singing in unison

'The Jews are dead . . . hurrah . . . hurrah . . . The Yids are gone . . . hurrah . . . hurrah!' After 800 years, on the night of 26 September 1941, Eisysky was 'Juden Frei'!

At the end of the old cemetery, in the direction of the church, stood a few Christian homes. Zvi knew their owners. He made for the nearest house and naked, covered in blood, he knocked at the door. A peasant opened it, holding a lighted lamp which he had pilfered that day from a Jewish house. 'Please let me in', Zvi begged. The old peasant took one look at him and shouted: 'Dirty Jew – go back to the grave where you belong!' And he slammed the door shut. The response from the other houses was no different.

On the edge of the forest lived an old widow whom Zvi knew well. He used to take her a bowl of soup and some chicken legs on Friday nights at the bidding of his mother – and she was always deeply grateful. Now she appeared at her door holding a burning piece of wood in her hand. Zvi pleaded to be let in. Her reply was to scream at him: 'Jew, go back to the grave at the old cemetery!' She chased him away brandishing the burning piece of wood in a threatening manner as though warding off evil spirits, crossing herself with her free hand.

'I am the Lord, Jesus Christ. Your saviour. I have come down from the cross. Look at me – the blood, the suffering of the innocent, the pain I suffered to offer you salvation! Don't you recognize me?' Zvi told her.

The widow fell to the ground, kissing his blooded feet, crying 'My God . . . my God . . .' and continuing to cross herself feverishly. Zvi entered her home and promised her that he would bless her children, her farm, and her – but only if she would keep his visit a secret for three days and three nights and not reveal it to a living soul, not even the priest. She gave her solemn pledge, washed him, fed and clothed him.

As he left he reminded her that the Lord's visit must remain a secret because of his special mission on earth. Wearing the farmer's clothing she had given him, Zvi disappeared into the nearby forest, met up with other Jews hiding from the Germans – and in this way the partisan movement was born just outside Eisysky.

The Lost Book

Recently, I attended a lecture organized by the '45 Group, a 'club' of adults who were all children of parents gassed or murdered by the Nazis. These children survived the Holocaust and were brought to England by a charitable English Jew and have since made good, married, created their own families and formed themselves into a sort of mutual aid society in which they assist the less fortunate members, take care of the families of those who have died, and donate large sums to various charities. They are a remarkable group of men and women who never let themselves forget that, but for a quirk of fate, they would now be ashes in the grate of the camp furnaces – like their parents before them.

The lecturer was himself a survivor of the Warsaw Ghetto and had a remarkable story to tell. It appears the Jewish doctors of the Ghetto decided to turn their misfortune to good account, and used to meet regularly to compare notes of the physical and mental effects of starvation and deprivation on their patients and themselves. A record was kept and all observations analysed and documented.

The book was buried and never found by the Germans. After the destruction of the Ghetto and the liberation of Poland, it was salvaged and fell into the hands of the Russians who have never published nor released its contents despite numerous official and unofficial approaches.

The contents of the manuscript could be of definite

assistance to medicine, being an account of data not previously documented in such detail.

We may never be privileged to study the material, but the remarkable fact remains that Jewish doctors, in the midst of deprivation and extermination, should have been so unselfish as to take advantage of their plight and offer to science the results of their first-hand experience.

Just another proof of man's faith in tomorrow and the will to survive spiritually and mentally, even though the body was being destroyed.

Lie in Front of that Tank

I met him in Israel: a sturdy sun-tanned senior citizen of a kibbutz where he had devoted his ingenuity to discovering how to grow plants and vegetables in the air without the need of soil: using a chemical spray and water.

His arm bore the number affixed to his flesh by the Nazis in Germany. I took out my notebook and pencil and asked him if he'd be willing to tell me of his sufferings there. He stared at me and said firmly:

'No, I will not tell you of suffering, but of death. Death and resurrection. When the Germans realized they were losing the war, rather than release us from the concentration camp, we were taken on a forced march hundreds of miles into the interior. Many died on the march, but still they made the rest trudge on. I was young then, and considered a strong worker, so the commandant was keen to keep me alive. But he was a sadist and took delight in singling me out for punishment on any pretext he could think of. Once I dared to beg him to stop beating an old man who had stumbled and could not rise.

'"I have not filled my quota of whip lashes today," he laughed, "so you may take your choice, Jew. Either I give it to him, or *you* can feel the sting. Which is it to be?"

'He knew what my answer would be . . . and he struck me across the face and chest in vicious delight.

'Day after day, when he wanted to punish an individual, he'd order me to step up and take the beating in the other's

64

stead. In the end I could take it no longer. I begged him to shoot me there and then and put an end to it.

'"You're not worth wasting a good bullet, Jew! Lie down on the road in front of that tank coming down the road and end your life yourself!"

'There was in fact a column of tanks coming in our direction. I limped to the centre of the road and lay down directly in the path of the leading tank. I said "Shema Israel . . ." and closed my eyes, praying for the end to be quick. I finished the Shema and I could hear the tanks passing, but I dared not open my eyes. I carried on saying any prayer I could remember. Somehow I didn't dare stop. Finally, when I looked up, I realized that they had all passed. What must have happened was that the first tank commander – seeing my body on the road – had swung his tank in a curve to avoid me, and all the others must have followed his lead.

'When I realized that God had inspired the commander to a merciful deed I was determined to repay His goodness by deserving the life He had given me. I had been closer to death with each tank – and survived. It was like lying in the path of eternity – and being resurrected!

'From that day nothing the commandant did could break my spirit, and he eventually tired of bothering.

'I survived the war – was rescued by the Americans – and here I am to prove it. Now write your story and leave me in peace. I have work to do. Shalom, young man.'

A Handful of Toffees

She looked so frail as she came out of the shop in Mea
Shearim, in Jerusalem, holding an alarm clock in one
hand and grasping the doorpost with the other. I tried not
to let her notice my curiosity as she carefully guided her
steps on the uneven pavement which was in the course of
being repaired. I offered her my arm for support for it was
dangerous for a woman as old as she to negotiate the
broken stones.

The paving slabs became more regular just before the
corner and she let go my arm with a quiet 'toda raba'
(thank you very much). I turned away and took several
paces forward, but I glanced back at her when I saw the
traffic lights ahead and wondered whether she would turn
right or want to cross the main road. Again I took her arm
and I noticed that she continued to walk as carefully as
though she were still treading on broken ground. I asked
her if she wanted to cross the road, but her reply left me no
wiser for she answered in Hebrew. I tried Italian but she
shook her head.

'Non, non . . . je ne parle pas l'Italien . . . malheureuse-
ment, jeune homme!'

I was pleased that, after all, we could converse in a
common tongue. We turned the corner and only a few
yards further on, she held me back as she crossed in front
of me and pushed open a pair of narrow, broken old
doors. She led me into a dark corridor with room only to
walk in single file. A few more paces and she placed her

foot on the first of the stone steps rising ahead to the next floor.

I bade her 'adieu', but she would not let go my hand. 'Non, non . . . venez avec moi . . . je vous en prie.'

I was surprised to see that she climbed the steps one foot ahead of the other with a sudden vigour which she had not displayed in the street. I suppose the familiarity of home ground brought back her confidence.

At the top, she removed a key from her handbag and unlocked the door. Again she grasped my hand firmly and drew me into the room. Then she locked the door behind us. This immediately worried me for I did not like the idea of being locked in the room with an elderly stranger, and I found myself growing tense. She must have sensed this, for she smiled at me and murmured:

'N'avez pas peur, jeune homme . . . je ne vous ferais pas du mal!'

I had to chuckle at the thought of this tiny old soul, so close to her grave, doing me harm and my quiet laugh put her at ease. She still had not let go my hand as she deposited the alarm clock on a small table, opened a wardrobe door and took out a biscuit tin, flipped open the hinged lid with her thumb in an expert manner, and then released my hand in order to dip hers in the tin and grasp a fistful of toffees which she thrust into my palm, accepting no refusal.

Then she offered to make me a glass of camomile tea. I declined and explained I must be on my way, but she did not accept this.

'Asseyez-vous . . . je vais vous demander un conseil.'

She seemed so determined, there was nothing for it but to obey. I sat on the edge of the bed and looked around me. The room was almost as narrow as the staircase, and contained only the bed, the little table and a wardrobe which must once have been an attractive piece of furniture. The evidence pointed to poverty, but the spotlessly clean bed-cover and the well-washed walls impressed me. A faded curtain enclosed a little gas cooker and a few shelves with utensils and crockery. As the old lady busied herself preparing the camomile, there was a knock at a door I had not previously noticed at the end of the room just behind the head of the bed.

The old lady glanced up quickly at me and I could see that her eyes had grown nervous behind her thick glasses. She gave me a penetrating stare which seemed to pierce deep into my being. When it was obvious that I too had heard the knock, she edged past me and unlocked the door.

'Je sense que je peus compter sur votre discretion, Monsieur. Viens, mon petit . . . n'ai pas peur . . . c'est un jeune homme qui a du coeur. Il ne te fera du mal. Viens . . . viens . . . Yeheskele.'

She put her hand through the doorway and drew into the room a strange little being. As he came out of the shadow, I couldn't avoid gasping. Before me stood a handicapped boy with the body of a child but the head of an old man. His eyes could not focus well and his head moved as though it were not firmly attached to his neck.

I tried hard not to show my reaction, but the woman was too quick for me.

'Don't show pity for him, Monsieur. His mind is handicapped, but he's probably happier than you.'

Her English was good and I was taken aback. Why had she not answered me in English in the street when I first spoke to her? I hadn't time to voice my question for she led the boy to the bed and sat him by me, talking to him the while in Hebrew in the gentlest of tones. When he was comfortable, she carried on preparing the herbal tea while she spoke to me.

'You must forgive my dreadful English, but I must try to talk in a language he doesn't understand for I wouldn't want him to be hurt by anything I say. People think he is silly in the head because of the way he looks, but you'd be amazed at the struggle to express himself which lies behind that crippled mind. Yeheskel understands almost everything I say in Hebrew, French and Arabic, and he has such love and gentleness in his soul that he deserves our understanding. I think the Almighty withdrew speech from him because if he could speak, his wisdom would make us blush.'

'Prends ça, prends ça, mon petit agneau . . .' she murmured to the boy as she spoon-fed him from a cup of milk.

'Do you see how he drinks without spilling a drop? He's a good boy and I love him dearly. It is dangerous for me to show him to a stranger, but you have shown much kindness and I sense you will understand my problem and not give me away.'

Give her away? I was truly intrigued now, and my writer's mind tuned in its memory computer as I sensed a good story.

She stared deeply into my eyes for a long moment, then she took a breath, sighed, and began:

'He is my grandson: my daughter's boy. We were all living in Baghdad, in Iraq where the Jews had been for centuries. My son was an engineer and had been offered good work in Germany – so he stayed there and sent money home regularly until Hitler started his anti-Jewish laws, and he was arrested and thrown into prison. They beat him badly and tried to force him to admit he was a foreign spy – and for that they would have hanged him . . . but he managed to escape while he was being taken to another prison – and after great difficulties he succeeded in getting back to Iraq and the family. Then the war came and we all had to escape from our own country and with the help of some good people we got to Israel and started our life again.

'My son-in-law would not leave me behind even though he had 11 children and a wife as well as his own mother to support. Oh he was such a good man! I couldn't have wished for a better husband for my daughter. I have trust in my God, but I will never understand why He should want to take a good man and his family – such strong, sturdy children – and leave only this useless old remnant and a boy who cannot help himself! But God's ways are God's ways and there must be a reason we are perhaps not permitted to know in this world. Do you believe in a world to come? Of course you must, for I see from your skullcap you are religious. I do – and I know one thing for certain. My Yeheskel has a free passport to that piece of heaven reserved for the truly good. I pray he will put in a word for me, in spite of my impatience and inadequacy. C'est vrais, n'est-ce-pas, mon petit chou?'

She pulled the boy's head against her breast and gently stroked his tousled hair as she continued.

'My son-in-law did not earn very much . . . he found work as a clerk in a government office and his salary was hardly enough to keep us all . . . which is why I refused to be a burden to him and I rented this little room. I do well enough, you know. I make repairs to people's clothes . . . and sometimes, God willing, I get some lace curtains to make or even a wedding veil . . . and I manage.

'My grandchildren often came to visit me and that is why I keep a tin of sweets in my wardrobe always handy, and I have no grandchildren left to give them to. My little Yeheskel doesn't like sweet things. N'est-ce-pas, mon âme?'

She hugged the boy almost fiercely, and it was not difficult to sense the tragic longing beneath her gesture.

'He is all I have left in the world, and I love him more than myself. If I were to lose him too . . . life would not be worth living (God should forgive me)!'

I was touched to realize how a woman who looked close to 90, clung to life with such tenacity and I wished I had had a tape recorder to capture the vigour of her voice and personality . . . but I never seem to have one with me at such golden moments.

'What happened to his parents?' I asked. Her eyes clouded over and she was silent for a long moment.

'You know we have bomb incidents frequently, when young men with a distorted sense of values revenge themselves on innocent victims for the wrongs they feel were done to their own people in the past. You may have read in the newspapers about a bus which was blown up by a parcel bomb left on the luggage rack. Twenty-seven people were on the bus and only a few survived. All Yeheskel's family, his father, mother, his ten brothers and sisters . . . all were on that bus . . . and not one of them survived.

'Yeheskel had been left with me while the family went on a short holiday to the seaside. The first holiday they have had since they came to Israel. I read and hear myself of such killings, but this sort of thing happens to others – never to your own family. But this time, the Angel of Death found my son-in-law's name inscribed in the book of life and closed the page too soon. And all I have left is this young son of my daughter, whose mind is locked in a body which cannot synchronize with his brain and nerves, and who will always need someone else to be his eyes and tongue.

'I was so afraid the authorities would consider me too old to take care of him that I decided to hide him here and pretend he had gone to his Maker together with the rest of the family. If they find him, they'll dismiss him as unimportant and they will put him in an institution, and I know he would never be happy there. They are so busy, how could they ever have time and patience to understand his needs and give him back even a little of the love he offers to others without expecting anything in return? He is no trouble, you know; he eats seldom and he never asks more attention than you can give him. God gifts those who are unfortunate with a quality others do not possess . . . and his gift is that he always senses your mood and can somehow manage to comfort you when you are sad and to give you warmth and sympathy when you most need them. I am full of years and ought to have gone long ago. I know now that God kept me alive to care for this boy, and I am grateful for the duty He has granted me. But I do not know how much time I have left . . . after all, I have no contract with God. What will happen to him when my turn comes?'

She stopped talking and looked directly at me with such appeal in her eyes that I knew what would come next and I felt ashamed at my instinctive reaction.

'I judge all men by their eyes, and yours tell me you are a person I can truly trust, or I would not be telling you my secret. Now I am going to ask you something very important. Something prompted you to offer me your arm in the street when I was nervous of the broken pavement. Maybe that something was the hand of God who sent you to me this day. Perhaps He was showing me that you are the one to take over when I am gone? Will you, kind sir, take this boy and care for him? I can tell you are a family man . . . I expect you have children of your own. Each new child brings his own luck and his own reward for your care. Please, please take Yeheskel with your own sons . . . and you will never ever regret it, I promise you. These handicapped children are closer to God than many others of His beings, and they create an aura of his goodness which sends out radiations of strength and joy to all who come in contact with them. It is the very gift of life I am offering you – do you not see that? Please, please, do accept . . .'

She came very close to me and took my hand between hers. I could sense the pace of her heart beating faster than normal and the amazing strength of her grip was almost painful.

I felt like a murderer as a voice I did not recognize as my own seemed to come from my throat.

'No, . . . No . . . I'm so very sorry . . . but that would not be possible. I'm returning to England in two days and without the authorities' permission I'd be stopped at the airport. They might think I had kidnapped your grandson. They'd never let him go with me. Do you understand, Madame? I'm very sorry . . . but it just wouldn't be possible. Believe me, he'd be better off in an institution where they'd take proper care of him. They have very good homes for these boys, really they have.'

To my shame, I was so taken aback by the impossibility of her suggestion that I found myself at the door, trying to get out of the room before I remembered that the old lady had locked it. She turned the key, then opened the door for me.

'Shalom, Monsieur. Thank you for your patience in listening to me. I understand your concern. Please, I implore you, do not give me away. I will find someone to take care of Yeheskel. It is clear God did not mean him to be you. Shalom, Shalom, Monsieur.'

A moment later I was in the street, walking towards my hotel.

I have thought so much about it since then. Did I really meet that old lady? Somehow I can't believe it and yet . . . I still have those toffees she thrust into my hand: those toffees which are always on my conscience.

Was I right to keep her secret?

He Has Never Failed Me Yet

Rabbi Smith of Chicago told me a remarkable story. About two months before the State of Israel was declared, he travelled there by boat on which he met a sprightly woman of 90-odd whom he saved from an accident as she nearly fell down a stairway on board ship. They exchanged the usual pleasantries which occur between travellers.

'Where are you from?'

'Chicago.'

'I, too. Are you travelling alone?'

'Yes.'

'Where to?'

'To Eretz Israel. Where else?'

'But where in Palestine?'

'I don't know. To Eretz Israel.'

'You have to know to which town you're going, otherwise the British authorities might not even let you off the boat.'

'I don't know. Just to Eretz Israel.'

'Have you any relatives there?'

'I got a nephew.'

'Where does he live?'

'Eretz Israel.'

'But where in Eretz Israel?'

'I told you – in Eretz Israel. I don't know exactly where.'

'What's his name?'

'Chaim Szokoll.'

'Does he know you're coming?'

'No. He has never seen me before.'

Rabbi Smith looked at the old lady in wonder. 'But how will you find him?'

'I have faith in God.'

'But, Madam . . . the British are very tough on immigrants. If you are not expected and there's no one to meet you, they might send you to a camp in Cyprus.'

'Listen, young man: I am 91 years of age – I survived several concentration camps when the Nazis tried to finish me off – but God's Angel of Death never looked in my direction. The good Lord has never failed me yet. He'll continue to look after me.' In the presence of such simple honest faith, one ceases to argue. Rabbi Smith held his peace.

Members of the Irgun had just blown up a ship which was due to be sent to Cyprus with hundreds of refugees destined to be interned and the British army was on the alert. When the ship carrying Rabbi Smith reached harbour, soldiers came on board with fixed bayonets, and everyone was ordered to have their papers ready and to alight one at a time as their name was called out.

Almost like running the gauntlet, each passenger had to pass between two rows of soldiers – followed by one whose bayonet was held at the ready.

Came Rabbi Smith's turn. He was not permitted to wait and accompany Mrs Szokoll, so he took leave of her, feeling greatly concerned for the old lady.

Half way down the gangway, he turned to speak to her, but was immediately prodded by the bayonet. 'Oh no, you don't – move forward!' said the soldier.

As his feet touched soil, a young man approached him. 'Rabbi Smith? I heard your name called out. I'm a newspaper reporter and my boss sent me to interview you.'

'Not here, young man – with a bayonet at my back. Give

me your phone number. I'll ring you when I get to my hotel and arrange an appointment.'

'OK. I'll write it down for you.'

Rabbi Smith glanced at the piece of paper the other man handed him and read the name Szokoll.

'Is your first name Chaim, by any chance?'

'Yes. How did you know?'

'Do you have an aunt living in Chicago?'

The other knit his brows in concentration. 'I think so, but she must be very ancient. Who knows if she's even alive now.'

'She's very much alive – she'll be following me down this gangway any minute now. Just you wait.'

At that moment, over the tannoy came the announcement of the next passenger's name, and aided by a helpful Tommy, Mrs Shoshana Szokoll, aged 91, stepped off the boat – into the waiting arms of her astonished nephew Chaim Szokoll.

The Lady of Faith looked in the direction of Rabbi Smith and smiled as she called out:

'I told you He wouldn't fail me!'

The Adoption

'Moshe, I know we can't really afford it, but I feel we must do something for those orphans they've saved from the Nazis. Don't be angry . . . I know we've hardly enough for ourselves, and it's not fair to expect you to work yourself to the bone to feed yet another mouth . . . but I always remember what my mother used to say: "each child brings his own mazzell – his own luck"!'

That was Raquel speaking to her husband in Jerusalem, and far from being angry or reproaching her, Moshe said:

'Very well, Raquel – let's go to the orphanage and choose a daughter.'

'No, Moshe. You know me: I'd break down and cry and want to adopt them all . . . and that would be disaster. You go alone.'

Moshe laughed. 'All right, Raquel. For my pocket's sake I'll go on my own, but you realize we'll have to tighten our belts a notch or two.'

Raquel was not put out. 'God will provide.'

Both of them had bitter memories of the Jew-baiting in Hitler's early days back home in Germany and had so often reproached themselves for not doing more to persuade Raquel's parents and sister to leave Germany with them when they crossed the border on that bitter December night; but her father, always the optimist, had believed that the German people would not suffer Hitler for long, and besides, he couldn't bear to leave his furniture business which he had built up from a market barrow to the most important store in town. Now, mother, father, sister, her sister's husband and children – all were ashes scattered in the pits of the gas chambers.

'If only I could have had children of my own,' Raquel sighed, 'but it was not to be. Some of us must be barren to counter-balance the population explosion.'

Moshe caught the bus to the building where the orphan children were housed temporarily, while Raquel busied herself preparing the corner of the living room which she screened off into a mini-bedroom for the little girl Moshe would bring home to lighten their lives. Raquel scrubbed the floors, hung the new curtains, bought flowers and splashed her housekeeping money on a beautiful roast chicken while her heart beat fast and her finger-tips tingled like an actress's before a first night.

Several hours later, Moshe returned. With him were – not just one – but two children.

'Moshe . . . what have you done, for heaven's sake? We can barely afford one . . . what made you bring two?' Raquel demanded.

'Raquel, don't be cross. I couldn't help it. When I saw the girl, I somehow felt she was absolutely right for us; but the snag was that she had a brother, and I just couldn't bring myself to part them. If you'd seen how they held on to each other, you'd have done the same. I just had to take them both.'

'But Moshe . . . how will we be able to feed them?'

Moshe smiled. 'Didn't your mother always say "each child brings his own luck"?'

Raquel was truly worried. She embraced the children, gave them each a plate of hot soup, then sat them on a sofa and, having no toys or children's games, gave them the family photo album to thumb through while she took Moshe into the bedroom to face him with realities.

'Moshe, it's just not possible. They're lovely children,

but on your salary it's out of the question. To begin with, we've no room in the flat for two more and who can afford a bigger place? How are we to feed and clothe them both? You must have been mad even to think of it. You'll just have to take them back to the orphanage and find us . . .'

Raquel broke off her sentence as from the other room came a frightening scream.

They both dashed into the room – to find the little girl pointing to a photograph in the family album and crying uncontrollably – 'Mutti . . . Mutti . . .'

The photo was of Raquel's sister who had perished in Auschwitz.

Somehow – on that day of joy in the outskirts of the old city of Jerusalem – a city which had known death and resurrection so many times since David chose it for his capital centuries ago – Moshe Greenberg had faced a sea of worried orphans and had selected the very children of his wife's sister.

It was as though the hand of God had pointed the finger – and smiled.

Iliena

'Please sir, may I have the day off to go to Haifa?'

'Why?'

'Because I have to meet the boat coming in.'

'Whatever for?'

'I'm not sure, but something inside me tells me I must.'

Joseph Millienu had escaped from Romania at a time when it was dangerous to be a Jew, and had worked in the orange groves in Israel while piecing together the threads of his broken life. But his happiness in reaching the Promised Land would never be complete until his wife Iliena managed to join him. When they were escaping, she had fallen off the lorry in which they hid, and he had been unable to prevent her discovery and arrest as the lorry crashed through the barrier and crossed the border under gunfire. That was five years ago, and he had not heard a word from or about Iliena in all that time. He did not know of her broken leg, of her hospitalization, of the five-years prison sentence.

He knew only that on this day, an inner compulsion made it necessary for him to go to Haifa to meet the boat.

As it came into the bay, the deck was overflowing with its human cargo of refugees heaped together like bandages on lint.

The people alighted and were met by officials who guided them from trestle table to trestle table, documented them, numbered them and placed them in trucks which took them to the tents and improvised accommodation in the transit camps. One thousand per day were arriving from the Arab lands alone, plus those from Eastern Europe: all had to be housed, fed, cared for by a new government in a new yet ancient land – *their* land: poverty-stricken, short of every necessity of life, yet happy with the pangs of rebirth of the Jewish nation.

Iliena knelt and kissed the earth, as did many of the others around her; but she obstinately refused to join the queues at the trestle tables to give her details and be sent on to the overnight camp.

'Mein Mann . . . Mein Mann ist hier . . .' was all she would say.

The more the officials cajoled, pressed and begged – the stronger became her resistance. She looked around the waiting relatives and curiosity-laden people who jammed the quayside, but to no avail.

Meantime, Joseph had arrived late at the dock and missed the alighting passengers. He pushed his way through the throng – staring, searching, scrutinizing.

Suddenly a cry rose above the din and the tears of embracing relatives:

'Iliena . . .!'

'Joseph . . . Mein Mann!'

That particular day in Israel, fate had grasped Joseph's hand and drawn him to the harbour – while stretching out its other hand to carry across hostile lands, on to an unseaworthy boat crammed to over-capacity, a woman old before her time, scarred with beatings, skinny with the starvation rations meted out in prison – but a woman with determination and certainty in her heart, and fate had thrust them together to complete the broken jigsaw of their lives.

On that day, in Haifa bay, there was performed yet another unexplained miracle as love re-flowered on the soil of Israel.

I Shall Not Lose Hope

Almost every other man you meet in Israel has an interesting tale to tell: a tale of survival.

Menachem had been in a Polish concentration camp under the Nazis and had made a pledge that, should he see the end of the dark tunnel, he would study to become a rabbi and devote his life to teaching the young the meaning of faith, for faith alone had prevented others saying Kaddish* for him.

He had witnessed so many of his companions be singled out for the one way ticket to the gas chambers, and each time he wondered why he had been spared. Far from elation, it gave him a feeling of guilt. The day finally came when he heard his name on the roll-call and he knew that death had to be faced with dignity.

He prepared himself calmly, but could not account for the strangest feeling in his veins that for him, this day would not end in ashes.

Outside the door to the 'final solution' he stood naked among the other men. His neighbour, Michael, spoke bitterly, blaming Hashem** for not showing His hand and permitting the endless slaughter of His 'chosen people'.

'How can you be so calm, Menachem? Why don't you scream or curse, damn you?' he asked.

'That would be offering up nails for my coffin, Michael.

---

* Prayers for the deceased
** Hebrew name for God

I have faith and even as I walk through the door, I shall not lose hope.'

Michael laughed bitterly. 'There you go again with your religious humbug! I tell you, God doesn't care any longer . . . and you'll soon be proving that for yourself!'

Menachem stared back at the other. 'Are you so sure, Michael?'

At that moment a German sergeant arrived with fresh orders and called out the names of three men who were told to return to barracks. One of them was Menachem.

Michael perished that day, but Menachem never discovered why he and two others were plucked back for survival. But then he doesn't question the actions of the Almighty. He merely recognizes His hand in that moment of mercy. Every time he loses patience or faces an unfair situation, he casts his mind back to the reading of the three names and to that instant when the Divine fishing rod caught him on its hook and cast him back on dry land.

Love Thine Enemy

It's a beautiful sentiment, but is it really possible in this day and age? To Signora Heinke Piattelli it is. This is the story of a remarkable woman and the events which led to her forgiving perhaps the greatest crime of all: murder.

The man whose path crossed hers so fatefully was born in Belgium in 1934. Raphael Blitz was only 6 years old when the Nazi armies invaded the country. His father was arrested and taken to a labour camp from which he never returned.

In order to save her boy's life, Raphael's mother had him baptized and cared for in a convent. They had been very attached and little Raphael missed his mother desperately. She was sent for and handed back the child. Without her he was wasting away. There followed months of hiding, of moving from district to district, of anxious nights in damp cellars, of narrow escapes from detection. Again, the woman was forced to beg the nuns to save her child, and yet again it was necessary for her to take him back to stop his pining. He was moved from convent to convent and finally, at the end of the war, he was transferred to an orphanage and later sent to Israel without his mother.

He had grown into a nervous, morose lad, suffering from chronic asthma. He had no companions and refused to make any. Embittered, lonely, tormented, Raphael could find no place for himself in the new land and eventually, hating everybody, he took to crime.

On 21 August 1957 Raphael attempted to rob the

Tsafon cinema in Tel Aviv. His plan did not succeed and the ticket seller at the box office sounded the alarm. Raphael grew panicky and in his attempt to escape, he shot and killed the ticket seller.

Fidia Piattelli, the murdered man, was an Italian engineer who had married a German Protestant brought up in Italy. During the war he had been interned by Mussolini's Fascists but was later released thanks to his wife's intervention. In 1945, they both left for Israel. They had no children.

Raphael was arrested and brought to trial. He was convicted of murder and sentenced to life imprisonment. At the Ramla prison he seemed more morose and strange than ever. He refused to associate with his fellow inmates, he was violent, troublesome and dangerous. He made various attempts to escape.

Psychiatrists attributed his behaviour to his unfortunate childhood, his lack of a father and more especially to his early separation from his mother whom he had adored. Had she survived, all this might never have happened.

Had she survived.

It was at this point that Heinke Piattelli, the wife of the murdered man, entered Raphael Blitz's life. She had been abroad at the time her husband died, and on her return she felt impelled to visit the prison and to meet the young rebel who had deprived her of her husband for the rest of her days.

The first meeting passed in utter silence. She merely studied him as he eyed her with apprehension. In that silence a bond was created between them: a bond of mutual loss, of sympathy, of understanding.

Heinke Piattelli became a regular visitor to the prison. Being a violin teacher, she knew the value of music as a therapy to troubled minds and she brought Raphael a gift of a guitar. She taught and encouraged him to play.

Before long, Raphael underwent a complete change in his behaviour. Not only did his love for music grow, but he developed an intense desire for study. He took a matriculation course and passed his finals in various subjects.

Eleven years passed since Heinke and Raphael first met and in that time his nature had entirely altered. Altered? Or returned to what it would have been had his childhood been normal and had he not been deprived of his mother at so tender an age?

Perhaps in Heinke he found a substitute for her and perhaps in Raphael, Heinke found a son she longed to have and was unable to conceive? Was the bond which grew between them not a measure of that true love of man for his neighbour? That love which understands forgiveness and knows how to bring repose and dignity to a disturbed mind?

I believe we have much to learn from Heinke Piattelli.

Raphael was eventually released from gaol, has since married and started a family, and has become an honest, productive and respected citizen.

Mummy

In Israel, I met a woman who told me a rather moving story. She was one of a number of orphaned children in Austria whose parents were entirely wiped out by the Nazis and the little ones were secreted in a nunnery for safety. Later, the nuns were concerned as to what to do with them and a kind Catholic priest undertook to care for them. He baptized the children and commenced to teach them the tenets of Christianity. He was convinced that they had begun to lose the memory of their Jewish upbringing. After the war a member of the Jewish Agency discovered the whereabouts of those orphans and came to claim them with the intention of transporting them to Israel. The priest refused to let them go, maintaining that the children were happy in their new belief and it would be cruel to confuse them with buried memories of extinct customs and traditions.

The representative of the Jewish Agency argued that, however distant or buried in the subconscious minds of those little ones, the seed of their parents' creed was still alive and would regenerate. Finally, the priest offered a suggestion, 'I will grant you five minutes to convince the children. If you succeed, you may take them to Israel. If not, you must accept to leave them in peace with me.'

The woman agreed and went into the dormitory where the children were resting. She gently called out, 'Shema Israel, Adonai Elohenu Adonai Ehad' ('Hear O Israel, the Lord thy God – the Lord is One' – the first prayer a child learns at his mother's knee and the one recited on waking and going to sleep and at the moment of departing this earthly existence).

One after another the little ones began to cry out a single word, 'Mummy!'

After that the priest graciously admitted defeat and the orphans were permitted to leave with the woman.

I Am Not Rachel

Rachel Kahn's parents had been among those gassed by the Nazis at Auschwitz and she was one of the few survivors among the children found by the Allies when the camp was liberated. Later she was adopted by a childless American couple and taken to live in Connecticut in the United States. She grew up as a happy, attractive young lady, well liked by everybody. Although a cheerful person by nature, she had always felt that something was missing. Even when among her best friends, she experienced a sensation of loneliness. Her adopted parents did not hide from her the fact that her real mother and father had perished in the concentration camp and they did everything possible to make her feel truly loved. Every now and then she would fall ill, but the doctors could find no reason for this except to diagnose symptoms of illnesses which they maintained she did not have. The unrest in her made it difficult for her to take vital decisions and she split with Shimon – her boyfriend – when he proposed marriage, for although she cared a good deal for him she could not bring herself to make up her mind on such an important matter. She began to wonder if there was something seriously wrong with her, but she was fearful of consulting a psychiatrist in case the reason for her unrest proved to be a serious disturbance of the mind.

Trying to explain her problem she could only say 'I somehow don't feel complete'. Shimon decided to take a trip to Europe to try to forget Rachel. After visiting Vienna, Prague, Budapest and Paris, he decided on the spur of the moment to cross the Channel and make his way to London. He made the rounds of the tourist attractions and was drawn to Trafalgar Square, in the heart of the capital. He was about to cross a road when the traffic lights turned red and at that moment he caught sight of Rachel walking on the opposite pavement. He called her name loudly several times, but she did not react. Impatiently he waited for the lights to change again, then dashed across and ran after her. He spun her round to face him and embraced her warmly.

'Rachel', he said, 'what on earth are you doing here?'

The girl looked astonished and pushed him away. 'Who are you? I don't know you. How dare you accost me like this!'

Shimon could not believe his ears. 'Rachel . . . it's me . . . Shimon. Don't you recognize me?'

'My name's not Rachel, it is Monica, and I've never seen you before in my life! Please leave me alone or I'll call the police!'

'But Rachel, we've been friends for months and I wanted to marry you. Because you couldn't make up your mind, I took this trip to Europe to try to forget you . . . but I can't get you out of my mind!'

Something about his earnestness, and the genuine emotion in his voice moved the girl and when he proposed that she should join him over a coffee and discuss matters, she was intrigued enough to accede. Shimon described their relationship, the fun they had always shared together and their obvious feelings towards each other. Monica was not aware that she had been an adopted child and explained that she was living with her parents in Golders Green in London, had never been to Connecticut and was even unaware of its whereabouts. Although the girl's hair, eyes and features were identical with Rachel's, Monica did not have the little mole on her right cheek which Shimon loved.

'Did you have your mole removed surgically?' he asked.

'I've never had a mole,' she replied.

She took her leave of him, after agreeing to exchange addresses for she found him pleasantly attractive and felt he had somehow made a genuine mistake.

Shimon was completely at a loss to understand the situation and he returned to the States, determined to get to the bottom of the mystery. He called at Rachel's home but she was not in. He then told her parents of his strange adventure in London. They stared at each other with an odd look in their eyes. Rachel's mother then told Shimon something that they kept to themselves all those years – that Rachel had a twin sister who had remained in hospital after being liberated from Auschwitz and was not expected to live. Perhaps after all she had survived and Shimon had met her in London. When Rachel returned, they admitted the truth to her about her real parents and told her of Shimon's visit that day.

Rachel turned pale. 'I must visit her' was her immediate response. Travel arrangements were made and within a week she found herself on the doorstep of Monica's home in the north west of London. As she rang the door-bell her heart beat fast and her hands felt clammy. Monica's parents opened the door and greeted her lovingly. Rachel explained she was not Monica and blurted out all that Shimon had related to her. The couple invited her in and the lady, after consulting her husband, told Shimon the truth about Monica. They had never told her that she was adopted, but they were aware that she had a twin sister but did not know if she were alive. Perhaps this girl before them who looked the image of Monica could be she.

When Monica returned, the couple asked Rachel to remain in the next room while they confided the truth to her. Monica was shaken and burst into tears. When she recovered her composure she admitted there had always been a strange suspicion at the back of her mind. She was a complete blonde with soft pale skin, whereas her 'parents' were dark, Mediterranean-looking and there was absolutely no resemblance between her and them. The floodgates were open and excitedly she began to ask questions and decided there and then she would go to the ends of the earth if necessary in order to find her twin.

'No need to . . . she is right here – in the next room!'

They called Rachel in and the two girls faced each other. After a moment's hesitation, with one accord they flung themselves into each other's arms, crying tears of joy. They sat next to each other, holding each other's hands, and both seemed to have developed verbal diarrhoea. They compared notes, laughed a good deal, discovered that on the occasions when Rachel – in the States – had felt unwell . . . at that very time Monica in London was going through a bout of illness – sometimes quite severe. They discovered they had so many things in common, their taste in dresses, in boyfriends, in hobbies and outlook in life.

Rachel returned to Connecticut, having made up her mind to marry Shimon after all – and before long Monica burned her boats in London and emigrated to the States to be near her newly found twin. There she met Shimon's younger brother; fell in love with him, and the four joined each other in a double wedding ceremony.

'Now', admitted Rachel, 'I finally feel complete!'

They've Burnt Holes in the Sky

I met him on a kibbutz. His name was Itai and he was 5 years old. Not tall for his age, fair, tousled hair and pale blue eyes. To get him to talk to me at all – let alone run the full gamut of his knowledge of English – was something of a triumph. To him, I was an outsider: a stranger who had no business keeping my guide, Haggai (who was his daddy), away from him for so long!

When I first saw Itai he was playing on the sandy soil with his young companions. Playing, but not smiling. With them, yet strangely aloof. As Haggai greeted him, he glanced up at the familiar face and quickly looked away again, ignoring Haggai's presence. I had seen my youngest child do this to me on my return from abroad: a sort of punishment for having been absent for a week or more. I waited, confidently, for I recognized the game and I knew the next move. It was not long coming. Suddenly Itai rose, opened his arms to Haggai and waited to be swung into the air. Man and boy did not kiss each other as father and little son are wont to do: instead Itai gripped his legs around Haggai's middle, placed his arms round the other's neck, and snuggled his head against Haggai's chest. This gesture of affection over, Itai jumped down, took Haggai's hand and pulled him away from me towards the beach. When he saw that I was following, he began to run, dragging Haggai as though he wanted to forge ahead too fast for me to catch up. Only once did his eyes meet mine – and the hostility troubled me.

Luckily I know a trump card which doesn't often fail. I ignored Itai and began slowly and quietly to clown with my tape recorder, giving it a 'life of its own': letting it talk back at me, hit me on the head, appear to spin me round in circles and finally force me to somersault and land on my behind in the soft sand. I sneaked a glance at the boy and knew at once that the thaw had begun. I did some more clowning and quite suddenly Itai came close to me and said in Hebrew: 'Come and see my cave.' He showed no pleasure – but when he took my hand in his free one (the other hand had not let go of Haggai since their first moment of contact), I knew I had been accepted.

Have you ever known the thrill of a child's approval after a hostile beginning? I hope so, for it is difficult to describe. It is something like seeing the sunset over a calm sea after the storm, or the awakening day express itself in pastel shades in a clear sky.

Haggai told the lad I had four children of my own. Itai searched my face with his large serious eyes, then began to gather shells in the sand as a gift from him to them – to 'the children of the clown'.

On the way back we met Itai's mother. I found it strange that she and Haggai did not embrace, but merely shook hands and exchanged a greeting.

'Shalom Haggai.'

'Shalom Hani.'

They spoke in Hebrew and Itai left me to hold both their hands in his. Then he led us all to the library to show me his classroom and sleeping quarters. There his friends were seated in a circle, listening to their teacher telling them a story. As soon as they heard I was a foreigner, they broke into a 'foreign song'. (No matter that 'Frère Jacques' was French. I was from 'abroad' and they knew a song 'from abroad'.)

I felt the need to reciprocate in some way, so I did some

more clowning, but I could not succeed in bringing a smile to the lips of one of the most beautiful children I have ever seen. A very dark Indian girl with huge eyes and brilliant white teeth. 'Another problem child,' I told myself and glanced at Itai who seemed proud of his new possession – this English jester who turned on his clowning act at the sound of song or a laugh from his companions. Itai grasped my hand and led me away from the group towards a small building set apart from the rest. In it were 22 framed photographs of young men: perhaps between 18 and 21, and two of older men: I would say around 30 to 35. Itai took one from the lower shelf and held it out to me.

'Abba,' he said. 'My daddy.' I glanced at Haggai who nodded and later filled in the gap for me.

'I'm only his adopted father,' he said. 'It's a common enough story here in Israel. You see, I was a member of this kibbutz and Itai's father, Aaron, was my best friend. He was a great one with the girls and when the kibbutz sent him to the city to study at university, Hani followed him and insisted on sharing his flat and caring for him. She knew Aaron would never marry her – but she loved him and that was enough for her. Suddenly she came back to the kibbutz . . . and eight months later Aaron visited us. He saw that Hani was big with child. His child. You see, Hani had left him when she realized she was pregnant because she didn't want to be a burden to Aaron. When he learned this, he disappeared for two whole days to think things over. Then he came back and asked Hani to be his wife.

'Three hundred guests were at the wedding, for Aaron was very popular; and we danced and sang throughout most of the night. Then the war came and the young men were called immediately. Both Aaron and I were paratroopers. I was lucky. I came back. Aaron did not. So Itai was born without ever having seen his father – and I became his guardian. I come to see him as often as I can and he treats me like his real father . . . but I can never make him laugh. Thank you for clowning. You almost made him smile. He's a serious boy . . . unlike his father . . . and he has his own way of working things out.'

When he was 2½, I took him to see an airforce display and when he saw the parachutes coming down from the sky he asked me: 'D'you know what those round things are up there?'

'They're clouds, Itai,' I said.

'Oh no, they're not. You see, the parachutes are angry because my daddy isn't there to jump with them . . . so they've burnt holes in the sky.'

I asked Itai if there was anything I could send him from London and he replied: 'Yes, foreign stamps.' A modest enough request from a serious boy of 5 who goes each day to the House of Remembrance to say hello to the photograph of his daddy. His daddy who he has never met, and who would in all probability be playing with him right now: leap-frogging on the sand, exploring the caves, teaching him about the fish and the sea, tucking him in at night and telling him a bedtime story, sharing the best years of his childhood – perhaps even gifting Itai with a brother . . . If only . . . If only.

The Ticket

'She fell down a few moments ago and no one gave her a hand,' said the cloakroom attendant.

I had just helped to lift an elderly woman from the floor to a chair. It was at a theatre in the north west of London on a Saturday night. The place was packed with people who had paid well to support a visiting foreign company performing in aid of charity. The curtain was due to rise at any moment, and the late-comers were too busy to notice the less spectacular drama taking place by the cloak-room.

I picked up the woman's glasses and scarf and put them in her open handbag. She closed it herself and it was then I noticed that only her left hand was able to move. The other lay inert in her lap. 'Mmm . . . a stroke,' I thought.

She must have been in her early seventies, grey-haired, face lined; her large, soft eyes staring vacantly from under lids which kept closing and opening slowly as though she were emerging from sleep.

I questioned her. No response. I tried French, Italian, Russian. Her only answer was to show me her theatre ticket. I placed my hand on her forehead and stroked her hair. Her lips broke into a smile – so sweet and trusting that in that moment she looked nearer 17 than 70.

The attendant phoned for an ambulance and returned with a young man. He recognized her.

'Oh yes, she came to the booking office this afternoon and could only speak German. Someone else understood a little and said the woman was anxious to buy a ticket. We had only a few expensive ones left and she seemed thrilled she was in time to buy one.'

The ambulance arrived and we helped her into the canvas chair the two men brought for her. As they carried her expertly up the stairs, she did not take her eyes off me.

Later, I checked with the hospital: she was comfortable but still unable to speak. Her handbag had revealed no name or address.

I went to visit her and tried to talk to her in my few words of German. Nothing registered. She stared vacantly and what emerged from her lips was mere sound without meaning.

Three days later, her identity remained as mysterious as the night of her collapse. No one had made enquiries about her, either at the theatre or through the police.

I visited her again and took with me a pot of red cyclamen. She was in a wheelchair, about to be taken for a walk. She sat immobile, lost, completely uninterested in her surroundings. I noticed her left hand was clenched.

I placed the flower pot on the table of her wheelchair. She accidentally knocked it over. I started to stand it upright again, but she pushed my hand away and straightened it herself, then felt the pot all round and touched the flowers rather as a blind person might, but with her fist still half clenched. She looked up at me and her eyes seemed for the moment less vacant. She attempted to speak, but again only gurgling sounds came from her lips. My heart went out to her. Imagine the torment that must go through such a mind – still partially active, still sending commands through the nerves to that part of her body as yet unable to react; a mind struggling to enunciate, to explain, to communicate, but wholly unable to.

Was she destined to remain unidentified? Anonymous?

She screwed up her eyes and the muscles of her face went tense. I put one hand on her forehead and caressed her hair with the other. She began to relax, then slowly smiled: the same trusting, ingenuous smile she had given me when I made that particular gesture the night I found her at the theatre. Had she recollected it? Had something finally clicked in the darkened recesses of her mind?

Eagerly I said in German, 'Sonntag . . . ? Theater . . . ? Verstehen . . . ?'

I think she did understand. She made a sign with her hand. I gave her paper and pencil. She took it between her thumb and forefinger and in uneven letters she began to write a man's name and an address in Hamburg. The silence had been broken.

The name she wrote proved to be her son's. He flew over to be with her and assist in her recovery.

He told me that they were both survivors from Hitler's Holocaust and had both been given refuge in England. He had gone back to Germany to try to reclaim the family business which had been taken from them during the anti-Jewish measures when they were sent to a concentration camp where his father had perished. She had vowed never to set foot in Germany again and had chosen to stay here awaiting her son's return.

But fate is cruel – or perhaps kind? That name and address were the last words she wrote. She died in her sleep two days after her son's arrival. Peacefully and silently. When they unclenched her fist they found in it the crumpled ticket for the Sunday night show she had wanted so much to see.

Perhaps the excitement of its anticipation had brought on the stroke in the first place. Perhaps she died, still believing she was soon to see the dancers and singers and dared not part with the expensive ticket she had bought – and her mind had stopped at that moment of happiness.

She was old and sooner or later death was inevitable. Perhaps after all she had picked a fine moment to buy her ticket – for the final journey to her Maker.

Love Every Half Hour

The following story was told me by my brother Ronald.

'At a reception I attended to raise funds for a hospital in Israel, the guest of honour was a high-ranking member of the Israeli parliament who spoke eloquently and persuasively. Many hands went to their cheque books and a generous sum was raised to buy new medical equipment, beds and an ambulance. I was very impressed with the speaker and could well understand the predictions voiced by the 'pundits' that, given a few more years of experience, the gentleman might find the path clear to the premiership.

'The name of the speaker and something he said about having been a patient in that very hospital as a child, stirred a distant memory, and quite suddenly I knew where I had seen him before.

'During my five and a half years service in the British Army in the last war and after, I had served for a short time in what was then Palestine. I had visited that hospital when it was a mere collection of huts and temporary dwellings, and in the children's ward I had noticed a boy lying asleep in a metal cot, sucking his bottle. Although he was curled up in a tight ball, as though he was attempting to relive his existence in his mother's womb, he seemed too old and too big for a baby's cot. Curious to know his malady, I glanced surreptitiously at the chart at the end of his bed – and saw only his name and the recommended treatment. It read: LOVE – EVERY HALF HOUR.

'I asked a nurse what that meant and she explained that

the boy was the sole survivor of a batch of Polish children who were found abandoned by the Nazis when their concentration camp was overrun by the British towards the end of the war. The German doctors in the camp had been conducting an inhuman experiment on the very young children: they had separated them from their mothers and kept them in confinement under the supervision of Aryan women who were forbidden ever to talk to them, to cuddle them or to show any interest whatever. This was an attempt to assess if the deprivation of love would stunt their growth and to judge how much of their normal development was due to the contact with the mother and to the love and attention given them by her.

'The results were disturbing. Generally the little ones communicated with each other by animal-like noises; others never uttered a sound. Many slept too much and became lethargic and lacking all energy. Most took to cuddling themselves with their arms clasped tightly across their chests and rocked all day long either from side to side or backward and forward. Some cried or hummed throughout their waking moments, and the majority gave up the ghost and died – not through lack of food – but of the hunger for love and attention.

'I can think of few more inhuman experiments man could perform on his fellow-being – and a helpless, tiny, dependent human being at that.

'When the British reached the concentration camp, the sole survivor of this particular batch of children was the little lad later taken to Palestine whom I had come across in the cot in the hospital. On arrival he weighed only 11 lb, had massive pneumonia, there was a deficiency in the number of thrombocytes and his extremities were becoming deformed. During treatment he stopped breathing, he turned blue and his heart stopped beating. He was revived by artificial respiration, at first from mouth to mouth, then with oxygen and cardiac massage. The results of lab tests showed that his body contained only 3 mg of calcium. By all the laws of nature when the serum shows under 7 mg a person usually goes into spasms and loses consciousness. It is generally accepted that one cannot live with less than 5 mg of calcium. The child had survived with only 3 mg of calcium: a rare medical phenomenon.

'When I saw him, he had already recovered from most of his troubles, but was evidently attempting to catch up with what he had missed both physically and psychologically as a baby, and that was why he felt most comfortable curled up like an embryo in a cot, sucking a bottle he ought long since to have discarded.

'The doctor who prescribed "Love – every half hour" was an inspired man and the regular cuddle, coo and caress paid dividends, for that child who defeated death in the concentration camp is now one of the most eloquent ambassadors for his country, a brilliant politician and, who knows, a prime minister to be?

'Such is the force of love. Love – and something else?'

Together

My mother Rachel, may she rest in peace, used to suffer badly from arthritis, and early in the last world war, she was sent to Buxton for spa treatment. In the hospital was a Polish immigrant who spoke no English and seemed extraordinarily lonely.

Roman had escaped from Poland and made his way across Europe and the Channel to join the scores of refugees who sought succour and a new life on our hospitable shores. During his escape he had lost his wife whom he had not seen now for three years – but an inner voice and faith told him she was alive and would one day arrive in England to join him.

My mother busied herself trying to lighten his worries, and pointed out that the cook happened to be Polish and could converse with Roman and interpret his requests to the nurses. Roman accompanied her to the kitchen – and gave a scream which penetrated the very marrow of Mother's bones, for the Polish cook was none other than his lost wife, Stefania!

There is an old Jewish saying: 'God creates them – and brings them together.' He certainly did on that day in Buxton, for Roman and Stefania.

A Morning Greeting

An eminent rabbi living in a small town near the city of Danzig was highly respected by Jew and Gentile alike. He was in the habit of taking a stroll through the city every morning, and insisted on greeting every passer-by – most of whom were familiar faces to him. He was meticulous about etiquette and insisted on addressing each individual by his proper name and title. He was known and admired by all and sundry and adults would point him out to their children for his smart attire, his long black overcoat over his well-tailored suit, his top hat and his silver-topped walking cane. 'That is a true German gentleman', they would say and add 'I pray that you will grow up to be like him.' On the outskirts of the city he regularly passed the property of an ethnic German by the name of Herr Muller. The rabbi would call to him as he worked his field, 'Good morning, Herr Muller' and Herr Muller would walk across his field, raise his hat and reply with a good-natured and respectful smile, 'Good morning, Herr Rabbiner'.

Came the war and Herr Muller donned an SS uniform and left the town. At the same time the Jews were rounded up and the rabbi lost his entire family in the death camp at Treblinka while he was transported to Auschwitz.

During the dreaded periodic selection, the rabbi stood in line with his fellow Jews as the officer walked before them, elegantly uniformed with immaculate white gloves and a little riding crop in hand, examining each body before him and calmly pointing either to the right or to the left – one way to a life of tortuous hard labour – and the other to immediate entry to the gas chamber. Dressed in the striped camp uniform, head and beard shaven and eyes feverish from starvation and disease, the rabbi looked like a walking skeleton. As his turn came, he recognized the face of the officer playing God – and he found himself addressing him as he was wont to do in that dim, not so distant past on the outskirts of Danzig. 'Good morning, Herr Muller.' The officer answered automatically 'Good morning, Herr Rabbiner' before he realized whom he was addressing. 'What are you doing here, Herr Rabbiner?' he asked in a friendly and surprised way.

The rabbi smiled gently. Did he really need to answer that question?

The officer changed the direction of his pointed whip from the left to the right. From death to life.

The following day, the rabbi was transferred to a safer camp. He survived to tell this tale.

Such is the power of a morning greeting!

The Loose Shoe-Lace

My friend Jean-Marc Vasseur's father was a German Lutheran living in France and married to a Jew. They had no children. When war broke out, he sent his wife to America for her parents had been arrested in Germany and never heard of again, and she feared for her own safety if the Germans were to invade France. Her fears were well founded for the Nazis, as we know, conquered France and immediately ordered the arrest of all Jews in the country.

A French collaborator denounced Herr Vasseur to the new authorities, declaring him to be an 'enemy of the Fatherland' and, although a German Lutheran, he was probably a potential spy because he was married to a Jew. The man was arrested and tossed on to a train full of Jews being supposedly 'displaced' to another region of France but in fact destined for the extermination camps in Poland.

Herr Vasseur had been arrested in the small hours while still in bed and was forced to dress so hurriedly that he was not given time to don his shoes. On the train he found himself close to a man with no jacket or overcoat and shivering with cold. He exchanged his warm overcoat for the other man's shoes. *En route* all the occupants were ordered to disembark and change to another train. As Herr Vasseur stepped on to the railway platform he bent down to tie his loose shoe-lace. A German guard kicked him to the ground and pointed a rifle at his head, probably intending to despatch him there and then – when he noticed the badge of a leader of the German boy-scout movement worn in the lapel of Herr Vasseur's jacket.

The guard hesitated, then asked: 'Were you a scout leader?'

'Yes.'

'Where?'

'In Einbeck before the war.'

The guard smiled. 'I'm from Einbeck. And I was a boy scout.'

The man looked rapidly to his right and left, presumably to ensure that he was not being watched, then whispered: 'Look . . . I'm going to turn my back . . . and I don't want to see you escaping or I'll be forced to shoot you. Now get going. Schnell! Schnell!'

Herr Vasseur bolted for all he was worth into the under-growth by the side of the open platform and once the train had departed with its unfortunate victims he took to the woods and escaped.

Somehow he managed to stay in hiding for the rest of the war. After France was liberated he made his way to the United States and rejoined his wife. In the first flush of their happy reunion my friend Jean-Marc was conceived and there he grew to manhood and eventually became a husband and father himself.

Jean-Marc told me that his father had placed that precious shoe-lace in a frame and hung it on the wall as a permanent reminder of how his life had been spared because of that loose shoe-lace and a sentimental German soldier still attached to his boyhood memories.

Five Babies

This story was related to me by Elbert Hubbard – a New York journalist.

'Riding on the Grand Trunk Railway going from Suspension Bridge to Chicago, I saw a sight so trivial that it seems unworthy of mention. Yet for three weeks I have remembered it, and so now I'll relate it, in order to get rid of it. Possibly these little incidents of life are the items that make or mar existence. But here is what I saw on that railroad train:

'Five children, the oldest a girl of ten, and the youngest a baby boy of three who were travelling alone and had come from Germany, duly tagged, ticketed and certified. The parents had bribed the authorities in Germany to allow the children out but, under Hitler's anti-Jewish laws, they themselves were prevented from leaving the country. The old lady was to meet them in Chicago. The children spoke not a word of English, but there is a universal language of the heart that speaks and is understood. So the trainmen and the children were on very chummy terms.

'Now, at London, Ontario, our train waited an hour for the Toronto and Montreal connections. Just before we reached London, I saw the conductor take the three smallest little passengers to the washroom at the end of the car, roll up their sleeves, turn their collars in, and duly wash their hands and faces. Then he combed their hair. They accepted the situation as if they belonged to the conductor's family, as of course they did for the time being. It was a domestic scene that caused the whole car to smile, and made everybody know everybody else. A touch of nature makes a whole coach kin.

'The children had a bushel-basket full of eatables, but at London that conductor took the whole brood over to the dining-hall for supper, and I saw two fat men scrap as to who should have the privilege of paying for the kiddies' suppers. The children munched and smiled and said little things to each other in Teutonic whispers. After our train left London and the conductor had taken up his tickets, he came back, turned over two seats and placed the cushions lengthwise. One of the trainmen borrowed a couple of blankets from the sleeping-cars, and with the help of three volunteered overcoats, the babies were all put to bed and duly tucked in.

'I went back to my Pullman, and got into bed. As I dozed off I kept wondering whether the grandmother would be there in the morning to meet the little travellers. What sort of disaster had deprived them of parents, I did not know, nor did I care to ask. The children were alone, but among friends. They were strong and well, but they kept very close together and looked to the oldest girl as a mother. But to be alone in Chicago would be terrible! Would she come?

'And so I slept. In the morning there was another conductor in charge, a man I had not seen before. I went into the day-coach, thinking that the man might not know about the babies, and that I might possibly help the little immigrants. But my services were not needed. The 10-year-old "little other mother" had freshened up her family, and the conductor was assuring them, in awfully bad German, that their grandmother would be there – although, of course, he did not know anything at all about it.

'When the train pulled into the long depot and stopped, the conductor took the baby boy on one arm and a little girl on the other. A porter carried the big lunch-basket, and the little other mother led a toddler on each side, dodging the hurrying passengers. Evidently I was the only spectator of the play.

' "Will she be there? Will she be there?" I asked myself nervously. She was there, all right, there at the gate. The conductor was seemingly as gratified as I. He turned his charges over to the old woman, who was weeping for joy and hugging the children between bursts of lavish, loving Deutsch.

'I climbed into a Parmelee bus and said "Auditorium Annex, please". And as I sat there in the bus, while they were packing the grips on top, the conductor passed by, carrying a tin box in one hand and his traincap in the other. I saw an Elk's tooth on his watch-chain. I called to him, "I saw you help the babies – good man!"

'He looked at me in doubt.

' "Those German children," I said, "I'm glad you were so kind to them!"

' "Oh", he answered, smiling. "Yes, I had forgotten. Why, of course, that is a railroad man's business, you know – to help everybody who needs help."

'He waved his hand and disappeared up the stairway that led to the offices. And it came to me that he had forgotten the incident so soon, simply because to help had become the habit of his life. There he was – big, bold, bluff and bronzed, his fair just touched with the frost of years, and beneath his brass buttons a heart beating with a desire to bless and benefit. I do not know his name, but the sight of the man, carrying a child on each arm, their arms encircling his neck in perfect faith, their long journey done, and he turning them over in safety to their grandmother, was something to renew one's faith in humanity.

'Even a great railway system has a soul. If you answer that corporations have no souls, I'll say: "Friend, you were never more mistaken in your life. The business that has no soul soon ceases to exist; and the success of a company or corporation turns on the kind of soul it possesses. Soul is necessary to service. Courtesy, kindness, honesty and efficiency are tangible soul-assets; and all good railroad men know it." '

Love Thy Neighbour

Nestling high up in the Apennine mountains in Northern Italy lies the town of Urbino: a delightful old town peopled by friendly men and women all of whom are on first-name terms with each other.

The Second World War was in full swing and Mussolini's government had thrown in its lot with Hitler. German troops were to be seen everywhere, and Urbino was no exception. Only a few Jewish families lived in the town and these were treated with respect and dignity by their Catholic neighbours who looked upon them as patriotic Italians – no different from themselves. However, the Nazis did not share their respect for the sons of Abraham and had sinister plans in mind. One day the *carabinieri* called at the homes of those few Jewish families and told them: 'We don't want to find you here early tomorrow morning . . . is that clear?' They had received orders from the Nazi authorities to round up all Jews and transport them to a concentration camp.

The Jews took the hint and all dispersed into the mountains. They organized it so that family A knew where B was hiding and family B knew only where family C was staying – and so on, like a relay race. As a result not one single Jew was arrested and all survived the war.

Those Italian Catholics had taken to heart the ancient Jewish commandment to 'Love thy neighbour as thyself'.

The Prediction

The year was 1943 and the German labour camps in Poland were in danger of being overrun by the advancing Russian armies. Orders were received from Berlin to liquidate all remaining Jews. The quickest way was to herd them into a barn and set the building alight. In Gardelegen camp alone eleven hundred men, women and children were burned alive in a devastating inferno. Only a handful were alive when the fire subsided but their lungs were badly affected by the smoke. These few men were then forced on to a truck together with inmates from another camp and driven to the woods to be shot.

'I am bored,' said one of the guards. 'Hey – you Jew boy, sing us one of your church songs.' The young man he addressed happened to have a rather beautiful voice and he chose to sing a Passover song. The melody is beautiful and easy to follow and soon other slave labourers of different nationalities and even the guards themselves joined in the singing.

As they reached the woods, the guard asked 'What's the meaning of that hymn?' The other translated the words for him:

And this is what has maintained our ancestors and us. For it was not one alone who rose against us to annihilate us, but in every generation there arose those who rise against us to destroy us. But the Holy One, blessed be He, ever saves us from their hands.

The German guard burst into a mocking laugh. 'Let's see how your God will save you from my hands!'

'I am still alive, but I'm not afraid to die,' replied the young Jew.

When they reached a clearing in the woods, groups of six at a time were taken to a ravine and shot. As the singer was taken to his death, the guard smiled with unpleasant delight. Suddenly there was commotion as a motor-cycle arrived carrying two high-ranking German officials. They gave orders that all remaining prisoners were to be taken back to the camp. Gardelegen had just surrendered to the American army.

Shortly after the liberation, the young singer died. His lungs had been irrevocably damaged by the Gardelegen fire. But he died a free man.

The Apple that Would Not Rot

Rabbi Aaron Waxman was a vigorous, athletic man who managed to keep himself fit even on the starvation diet irregularly doled out to the inmates of the labour camp. Before the Germans had brought darkness upon his land, he had been the minister of a small Jewish congregation with so few members that they were unable to pay his salary and he was forced to support himself and his family by practising his previous profession as a master carpenter.

He was chosen by his German 'masters' to lead a group of Jews to fell the trees of a wood just beyond the confines of the camp in order to extend the grounds. So as to create a regular rhythm as they worked, Rabbi Waxman would sing Hebrew and Yiddish songs in his melodious voice and enjoin the others to raise their voices with him. Even the guards enjoyed those melodies and encouraged him to continue. The electrified barbed-wire marking the confines of the camp had been taken down temporarily while the work was in progress and many armed guards lined the perimeter to ensure that no inmate could escape. One or two had made an attempt only to be gunned down the moment they set foot beyond the confines of the labour camp.

Although Poles living in the surrounding area were normally forbidden to go anywhere near the camp, the commandant decided he would take advantage of their curiosity and permit them to approach within a short distance as he wanted to prove to them how well-treated the Jews were by the Germans. In order to give the lie to the

116

rumours that were circulating, the inmates were instructed to carry a water-bottle and picnic bag on their shoulders to make prying eyes believe the men had ample food and drink with them while they worked – although closer scrutiny would have shown that the bags were filled only with old newspapers to make them appear full, and their water-bottles were completely empty.

On one occasion, a small Gypsy boy and girl tried to get near the perimeter and one of the guards showed friendliness toward them by offering them sweets and chatting to them patronizingly in his faulty Polish. The following day the two children returned, and this time they were munching apples. The Jews looked longingly at the red, juicy fruit and the boy must have sensed their hunger. He looked at their expressions, then at the apple he was munching and spontaneously hurled it towards the Jews. Several emaciated hands eagerly stretched towards it and a fight ensued until the strongest proved the lucky winner. Guards shouted at the children that it was forbidden to feed the men and shooed them away. The following day they were back again and one of the guards threatened to shoot them, but was stopped by another who urged him to let them alone as long as they did what they were told. 'Why are you soft with them, Pauli?' the other asked. 'Don't you know the Führer has declared them expendable? If I had my way I'd hang the lot of them. Gypsies are as bad as the Jews. Sooner or later we'll be rid of them altogether.'

Day after day the little boy came back to stand and stare for hours on end. Rabbi Waxman noticed that he had the features of those suffering from Down's syndrome. His face was flat and expressionless – almost Mongoloid, but his eyes appeared to show compassion, and Rabbi Waxman was moved to tears as he recalled his own small children whom he had not seen since the family had been arrested and parted from each other.

One day, when the boy noticed the guards were not looking in his direction, he tossed a fresh apple directly at Rabbi Waxman who caught it and quickly hid it under his shirt. Then the boy ran away and was not seen again for many days. Rabbi Waxman took care of that apple as though it were his most precious possession, which in fact it was. He decided not to eat it immediately but to keep it hidden for the imminent Jewish festival, and then to share it with his immediate companions as a glorious treat. He examined it daily to ensure that it was not beginning to perish, and was astonished to notice that it never changed colour and seemed to remain as firm and as fresh as the day the boy gave it to him. He said a silent prayer that the Gypsy boy should not fall victim to the Nazi atrocities like the rest of them.

Realizing that there was no change in the appearance of the apple, it appeared to him like a symbol of life and hope and he was convinced in a strange way that – as long as that apple did not perish – his life would be preserved. He longed for the boy to appear again and to be able somehow to convey his gratitude but either the child's parents would not allow him to return or – God forbid – the Germans had removed the Gypsies from their encampment and maybe by now they had shared the fate of the Jews.

Before the work of clearing the trees and laying down concrete prior to erecting new huts to house a further consignment of human fodder, the Russians had advanced rapidly and the camp commandant received orders to abandon the area and move the Jews many miles back into German territory. In the confusion, some of the Jews managed to escape – and among them, Rabbi Waxman, who took with him his precious apple.

To his astonishment, even after several months that apple still showed no signs of ageing and appeared to have a charmed life. This confirmed his belief that, as long as that apple did not deteriorate, his life would be spared.

He constantly recalled the compassionate look in the eyes of that boy who stood there hour after hour, staring at him as he worked on felling the trees: he felt true love for that handicapped child who had so generously given him that apple. Rabbi Waxman told me that after the war, he returned to the area in search of the Gypsy family – but they were no longer there and no one seemed to know where they had disappeared to. Some even denied that they had ever existed – but that unperishable apple was proof that neither it nor the boy were figments of Aaron's imagination. He had brought it to show to other survivors during their annual convention in Jerusalem and – believe me – the rosy hue on its skin seemed to emanate a mysterious glow. As one person observed: 'It must have been touched by the Hand of the All-powerful one above.'

Whispers from Beyond

Many people claim that in their dreams, deceased parents or relatives have visited them and given them advice on solving disturbing problems or predictions of calamities to come and how to avoid them. I call these visitations 'Whispers from Beyond'.

The following are some of the stories people have told me, or experiences I have had myself.

I Asked for Wonder

Inmates of Auschwitz death camp constantly asked themselves, if the Almighty exists, how can he allow the Nazis to make them suffer and slaughter them as they had been doing? It was decided to hold a court of justice and to try God for not raising his hand to save them.

The court was convened, a judge appointed and men were chosen to prosecute and to defend. After hearing all the evidence for and against, the judge pronounced his verdict: God had been found guilty. He then turned to those present and announced: 'Now gentlemen, it is time for the evening prayers.'

Even those with the strongest faith have in moments of despair cried out: 'Please God – if you really DO exist, show me a sign.' And yet – if he does decide to grant that wish in the manner in which he chooses, do we always recognize that gesture?

I remember my mother – in answer to my own doubt – cut out a quotation she came across and pinned it to the wall of my bedroom. It ran:

The man whispered, 'God, speak to me'
And a meadow lark sang.
But the man did not hear.
So the man yelled, 'God, speak to me'
And thunder rolled across the sky.
But the man did not listen.
The man looked around and said 'God, let me see You'

And a star shone bright.
But the man did not notice.
And the man shouted 'God, show me a miracle.'
And a life was born.
But the man did not know.
So the man cried out in despair:
'Touch me, God, and let me know that You are here!'
Whereupon God reached down and touched the man.
But the man brushed the butterfly away and walked
on . . .

In my prayers I once made a heartfelt request. I asked for wonder, and to my chagrin there was no response. I should have realized that God is not always silent and man is not always blind. As Abraham Joshua Herschel says: In every man's life there are moments when there is a lifting of the veil at the horizon of the known, opening a sight of the eternal.

Each of has at least once in his life experienced the momentous reality of God's existence. Each of us has once caught a glimpse of the beauty, peace and power that flow from the Eternal directly into our being. But such experiences are rare. To some people they are like a shooting star, passing and unremembered. In others they kindle a light that is never quenched. In every snapshot of our lives the obvious and the hidden sit side by side, awaiting only the sharpening of our inner lens to reveal its darkest secrets.

We dwell on the edge of mystery and ignore it. We fail to listen to the pulse of wonder. Some men go on hunger strike in the prison of the mind, starving for a sign from above.

Let me tell you a true story which almost belies belief. It concerns the Kabbalah – the ancient Jewish mystical interpretation of the Bible, studied even today by many Jews and Christians alike.

My son Jonathan studied in Jerusalem for over five years, and his best friend in the yeshivah or house of learning was a young man called Ben Buchwald. One day Ben received a phone call from his mother in Brooklyn, New York, to say she was going into hospital to have an operation performed on her knee.

Ben's mother had lost her parents, brothers and sisters in the Holocaust and was the sole survivor of her entire family. But it had taken great toll on her health. After the war she had married and given birth to Ben to whom she was truly precious. He doted on her and was greatly concerned for her well-being. When she told him on the phone of her pending operation he became panicky and immediately said: 'Mom – I want to be there when they operate. If I catch a plane tonight . . .'

His mother cut him short. She wouldn't dream of interrupting his studies. 'Just pray for me,' she said.

It is customary among religious Jews to say prayers at the grave of a great rabbi when they are particularly troubled, and Ben decided to do so for his mother at the tomb of Isaac Luria, a renowned and learned man of the fifteenth century whose grave has become and remains a place of pilgrimage for successive generations. Ben began by reciting Psalms but his Hebrew was still weak and the words wouldn't come easily. He closed the book, looked up at the heavens and spoke directly to the Almighty: 'Master of the Universe. I know You're very busy, but I'd appreciate it if You could perhaps send the soul of Rabbi Luria to the operating theatre to guard my mother.'

Late Saturday night when the sabbath was over on both sides of the world, Ben telephoned his mother at the hospital.

'How did it go, Mom?' he asked.

His mother sounded cheerful. 'I feel fine. They gave me a local anaesthetic and I didn't feel a thing, even though I was

125

awake the whole time. But something strange happened. I know you'll think I'm crazy, but during the operation – suddenly out of nowhere – a lion appeared and started walking around the room. It came right close to me and I was able to feel his fur. The funny thing was, I wasn't scared. I mean – there was that huge lion walking around – but I knew somehow that it was friendly. I felt as though he were guarding me from danger. I really felt safe. I asked the surgeon: "Did you know there's a lion here?"

'He looked at me as though I were mad! "What do you mean?"

'"Don't you see the lion, doctor?"

'"No – I don't see any lion. Listen, Mrs Buchwald . . . I'm very busy here, trying to concentrate on this complex procedure. I don't have time to look over my shoulder to see if I'm being attacked by a lion!"

'The doctor then told the anaesthetist to give me an injection to put me out. But when I woke up three hours later, the lion was still there, sitting in the corner and guarding me. I felt as if something were trying to enter the room, and the lion was keeping an eye on me and protecting me.'

Ben humoured his mother, but dismissed the story as being the effects of the anaesthetic. However he could not get it out of his mind. He called on his rabbi and recounted the whole story of his having prayed at the grave of a revered rabbi and his mother's crazy hallucination about the lion in her room. The rabbi remained deep in thought for a long moment, then asked:

'Whose grave did you go to?'

'Rabbi Isaac Luria.'

Ben's rabbi turned pale. 'You asked that the spirit of Rabbi Isaac Luria should be present to look after your mother – and you say a lion appeared? Did you know that Rabbi Luria of blessed memory was nicknamed 'Ha'Ari?'

'Yes', said Ben, 'but I didn't know what it meant.'

The rabbi smiled. 'It means the Sacred LION!'

This incredible story does not end there. Ben telephoned his mother again. 'Listen, Mom, did you happen to know what time it was when you first saw the lion?'

'Yes, actually I do remember. There was a big clock in the operating room, hanging right in front of me. It was twenty minutes after eight when the lion first appeared.'

Ben felt a surge of excitement as he worked it out: it had been 3.20 in the afternoon when he had said his prayer at the grave of Rabbi Luria. With the seven-hour difference in time it would have been exactly 8.20 in the morning in New York.

Go to Cairo, My Son

Paul Gryn was a young Czech engineer living in Prague at his mother's home when the Germans invaded their country. His father had died a few years before and his mother, knowing that the family was Jewish, had anticipated the storm clouds which had been gathering, and made arrangements with friends in France to accept their son into their home should the need arise to flee Czechoslovakia.

When the announcement came over the radio that the Germans had crossed the border, she told Paul: 'My son, the time has come to escape and make your way to this address in Paris. I have matters to attend to and will join you as soon as they are settled. Here's some money – now go with God, my beloved son.'

Paul was reluctant to leave her, but he could see the logic of her advice: it was useless to persuade her to leave with him. She was adamant that she could not go yet so Paul obeyed her instructions and embarked on the arduous journey out of the country.

Unfortunately, the moment the Germans entered Prague, they commenced rounding up the Jews and packing them off to concentration camps. Paul eventually reached Paris, but found it impossible to make contact with his mother. Before leaving his homeland, Paul had told his fiancée that he would send for her and his mother as soon as he was settled in Paris. He had known Ruth since their schooldays and she was desperate at the thought of being left behind, but she was not prepared to abandon her ageing parents. That very day Paul had purchased the wedding ring he had planned to place on her finger on their nuptial day. Instead he suggested that she accept it now as a token of his undying love, but she insisted he keep it until they would both be able to marry in the traditional manner.

Tearful, hurried departures are an agonizing wrench for anyone in their situation. All contact was now severed and Paul was not aware that his mother, Ruth and her family were among the first Jews to be arrested and deported by the Nazis. Paul joined the free Czech militia being formed in France and before long was locked in battle with the German army. He survived the war and immediately started searching for his dearest ones, but that path led to a dead end. The only information he succeeded in obtaining was that his mother had died in the concentration camp and that his young bride had been recruited among the able-bodied women forced to work for the Germans as slave labourers. He prayed that she would not succumb to the starvation and destruction which took the lives of so many millions.

One night his mother appeared to him in a dream and told him: 'Paul, my son . . . go to Cairo in Egypt.' This same dream occurred several nights running and Paul felt that this instruction must not be ignored. He made his way to Cairo, not knowing where he should go, or even why. He booked into a small pension and called at the offices of the Jewish Aid Agency. They had no knowledge of his family and fiancée and were unable to give him any assistance. Walking through the busy streets in the centre of town he noticed a commotion where someone appeared to have fallen and people gathered round to offer help. His heart-beats suddenly gained pace and he sensed an excitement for which he could not account. As he reached the young woman lying on the pavement, he gasped for there before him lay Ruth, his fiancée. When she was able to speak, she told him she had recognized him from the other side of the road and ran across, narrowly missing the oncoming traffic and was hit and knocked down just as she reached the kerb. An ambulance soon arrived on the scene and she was whisked off to the nearest hospital where fortunately the doctors found she had not sustained any serious damage other than a fractured arm and bruised hip.

A flood of words passed between the young couple as each tried to explain what had happened to them during the war years and what had brought them both to Cairo on this fateful day. Paul noticed that his beautiful fiancée now had a very twisted foot and he insisted on knowing what had brought that about. Ruth was at first reluctant to tell him, but he drew the truth out of her. It appears that the camp doctor had taken a fancy to her and tried to make her his mistress, offering her special favours, extra food rations and a decent bed to share with him. She had refused his advances and he turned vengeful. He forced her to undergo an operation in which he deliberately broke her ankle and reset her foot in a twisted fashion. 'If I can't have you, then I'll make sure you are unattractive to other men!' he declared.

Ruth was so ashamed of her appearance and the awkward manner in which she was forced to walk (Paul had always told her that she had such beautiful small feet) that she made no effort to trace him after being released from the camp, fearing that he would no longer want to be married to a girl with such a distorted and crippled foot. After her release, a distant relative of the family's living in Egypt had insisted on her going to live with them in their home in Cairo – where she was now staying.

Paul's reply to her fears about him changing his mind was to take from his pocket the box with the ring he had treasured all this time, and to place it on her finger as he said: 'I once saw a lovely play by a Welsh writer called Emlyn Williams in which he said to his beloved: "You have one very twisted foot, my darling wife . . . but the Venus de Milo was mutilated too." '

The Talking Cat

Joshua Sinclair, the eminent American writer and film director, told me two amazing stories.

When he was still a child in Germany, his grandfather was arrested by the Nazis and sent to Auschwitz concentration camp where unfortunately he perished. Joshua's parents had divorced and his mother managed to escape from Germany and took him to America. She was so traumatized by events and by the loss of her husband that she abandoned the child and journeyed to the Far East in search of spiritual comfort and a mystical philosophy of life. Joshua did not see her for eight whole years.

He was then studying medicine, and Joshua happened to be in his lodgings when a cat climbed into the room through the open window. He heard the cat say quite distinctly, 'You've to phone your mother.' Joshua had not been feeling well of late and he decided the voice was merely a figment of his imagination or a delusion of his sluggish brain. But the cat repeated its statement more insistently: 'You've to phone your mother!'

Joshua presumed he was more unwell than he had thought, nevertheless he decided to do as the strange voice had dictated. The first words his mother uttered as she answered the phone were: 'Did the cat tell you to phone me? I sensed you were not well and I wanted to advise which herbal medicines to take to get you well again.'

The other amazing story he told me concerned his deceased father. Joshua was now working as a journalist in the office of a newspaper in Europe. The war was raging and the air-raid sirens had gone. Joshua ignored this and remained at his desk when a colleague of his popped his head round the door and called out: 'Someone has just rung. He gave no name but said you were to phone your father immediately. He made it sound really urgent.'

Joshua was taken aback for his father was no longer alive. Curious to know who was the stranger who instructed him to ring a dead man, Joshua made for the telephone at the end of the corridor. As he reached it, a loud explosion rocked the building and the lights failed. The telephone no longer functioned and Joshua was knocked to the floor as a bomb ripped through the building. He was unharmed and he returned to his room to find that the ceiling had collapsed on to his desk. He realized that had he still been there when the bomb fell, he would probably no longer be alive.

Whose was the mysterious voice which insisted he leave his desk to telephone his deceased father? Was it the voice of a human being, or a veiled warning from a celestial body of the imminent danger? Joshua will never know, but these two experiences and his brush with death have strengthened his faith and belief that a hand greater than ours guides our destiny and protects us in time of danger.

Advice from Above

The widow Esther Kardysz and her 6-year-old daughter Florette managed to hide in a pit below the house of a Polish neighbour when the ghetto was liquidated. Esther's husband, parents and other members of her family had been shot by the Nazis before her very eyes, and she and her little daughter were the sole survivors.

The pit was dark, overcrowded, and the ground was covered with damp straw which gave off an unpleasant odour and was ridden with lice. Esther's whole attention was focused on saving her daughter. She gave most of her food to the child and she herself survived on scraps and morsels. An abscess had developed on one of Esther's teeth and she was in great pain. She tried hard not to let Florette see this, but the child was too sensitive not to realize her distress.

Esther's mother appeared to her in a dream and said to her: 'Why is no one doing anything to help you? Now listen carefully and do as I tell you and you will recover.' She then instructed her carefully on what to do to relieve her condition. Esther then passed on the information to the other occupants of the pit who acted accordingly and within a few days, the swelling had receded and with it the pain.

'You see, my dearest,' Esther told her daughter, 'Grandma will not allow anything bad to happen to you and me. She will always take care of us.'

Both mother and daughter survived the war and the Holocaust and lived to recount this story.

Avremele, Listen to Your Mother

Abram Grinberg was a young Jewish tailor living in Jezierzyce, Poland. When the Red Army retreated before the advancing Germans, he managed to join them for he knew what fate awaited him if he were to be caught by the Nazis. Later his unit was split into two groups. One group of volunteers was to be sent to Siberia and the other to join the forces already in combat. Offered the choice, Abram decided on the latter.

That same night his deceased mother appeared to him in a dream and told him in a decisive tone 'Avremele – you are going to Siberia!' She repeated this several times.

'But, mamma, I have already signed on to join the fighting unit.'

'Avremele – I've told you . . . you are to go to Siberia!' his mother insisted.

The following morning, Abram reported to his commanding officer and requested permission to change his mind. The officer reluctantly agreed.

Later Abram Grinberg learned that the entire combat unit he had at first decided to join had been wiped out at Stalingrad.

Returning Home

My friend Paul, his mother and father had lived in Vienna where the father had a successful furniture store. When Hitler invaded Austria, welcomed as a hero by the majority of the population, Paul's father was arrested and sent to a concentration camp and never heard of again. Anticipating the worst, he had made arrangements for his wife and child to flee Vienna should the worst come to the worst. After he was taken, his wife and child following his instructions and with the help of friends managed to reach England and safety. They arrived penniless, having left everything behind in Vienna. She eked out a living working as a daily for different families and when Paul eventually married, she insisted on living on her own in order not to be a burden on her son and his new bride. At 75 and weak with a heart complaint she begged Paul to let her go back to Vienna by herself 'for a holiday': but the doctors advised against this journey and Paul refused to allow her to take the risk.

She gave him no peace until he finally bought her a ticket and saw her off on the plane. As she embraced him, her voice was very moved and her eyes held his gaze in a long look which seem to signify gratitude, adoration, pride and sorrow.

Paul felt strangely disturbed as he drove home and a premonition gripped him with regret and anger at himself for allowing her to go.

Two days later he learned that she had died suddenly in a Vienna hotel. She left a note asking to be buried in the local cemetery near to her own mother. It transpired that for years she had been sending her small savings regularly to Austria to pay for a plot in the cemetery where her mother had been interred. Paul was happily settled with his wife and a child was on the way. She belonged to his past and was too old to have a share in his future. Her one desire was to make her final resting place close to her own mother to whom she had been devoted, and to whom she felt more and more drawn in her declining years. In her note she begged Paul not to mourn long but to get on with his life. During the weeks before she left London, her mother had appeared to her several times in her dreams, smilingly telling her her time was near and that they would soon be together again.

Manasseh

If ever you find yourselves in Avignon, that medieval French city of the popes, take a car-ride 15 km out to the little town of Carpentras.

'Why Carpentras,' you may ask, 'it's barely mentioned in the guide books? What is there that's special about it, except perhaps the Roman arch which has no unusual feature to recommend it?'

No, it's not the arch which should draw you to Carpentras. It is another link with the past – a small synagogue, built 600 years ago. Once it was the centre of a busy community of shopkeepers, tailors, craftsmen and tradesmen. Today, only 21 Jewish families remain.

Last summer, I paid a visit to Carpentras and called at the synagogue. I sentimentalized over the once-white walls, the worn wooden benches, wrought-iron candelabra, the minister's platform above my head, the women's gallery behind the criss-cross screen, the enchanting little circumcision chair hanging on the wall, the 25 Scrolls of the Law (one and a quarter to each family), and something within me grew sad. Here was my past, here my people had gathered every Friday eve to welcome the sabbath bride, here countless cantors had led their congregations in prayers of thanksgiving and praise; those wooden benches obtained their shine from innumerable coats, inadvertently polishing the seats as their owners rose and sat as the liturgy demands.

I followed the stone steps down to the well deep in the

bowels below, and found myself next to the *mikveh* – the ritual bath. The beadle was acting as guide to a small group of Frenchmen, Spaniards and Americans.

'Here come the women for their monthly purification, and here the good earth thrusts forth its liquid freshness in a limpid, pure stream, look, my friends – it is so clear that you can see your faces reflected below . . . hold that child, please, the steps are dangerous, and the water is deep!'

'Did the Germans close the synagogue during the war? Did they take away the Jews?' an American asked.

The guide was reluctant to say. 'I . . . I was not here. Come now with me to see the synagogue. Ah, we have a new visitor. Won't you join us?'

'Thank you, I have already seen it,' I told him.

'Then if you'd like to wait here, I'll return shortly and show you the bakery.'

'Thanks. I'll wait.'

Their footsteps echoed slowly away and I sat alone in the cool, stone cellar. Alone with the ghosts of my past.

Recalling Dr Brunler's theory, I am convinced that each of us bears his own aura, a form of radiation which affects everyone with whom we come in contact, and that every single thing we touch bears the imprint of our personalities for as long as there are people sensitive enough to receive these vibrations. I believe that we can conjure up a feeling and an atmosphere which has clung to the rooms, the walls, the furniture of the people who once loved, touched, breathed, laughed and suffered in those rooms. Because of this, when visiting a new place, I often sit in silence, with eyes closed, my finger-tips touching the furniture which once supported other beings, heard other tongues, shared other secrets. I let my mind relax – hoping to sense, if not receive, some of the radiations those personalities of the past have left around me.

On this occasion I sat on a stone bench, and my fingers

wandered into the crevice between the back of the seat and the wall. It encountered something smooth and hard. It was a small stone, almost perfectly round, which rested in my palm like a tiny creature, nestling for human comfort.

I closed my eyes and let my senses drift in search of the radiations. Did I sleep? I don't know, but in the corner of the cellar, I could dimly make out a shape emerging from the shadows. A long cotton coat hanging loosely on bowed shoulders; pale, hollow cheeks and wispy beard beneath a black round-rimmed hat, and from the sunken sockets there shone a pair of translucent eyes – gentle, dreamy; totally in contrast with the man's general appearance.

He stared at me for as long as I dared hold his gaze, then beckoned me to follow him as he turned – and merged into the wall!

Was I dreaming? I hadn't moved, yet my body seemed to leave me behind as it started forward in response to his gesture.

Once through the wall, I found myself in a classroom where some thirty boys were at their wooden desks. All wore hats and the side-burns of ultra-orthodox students. Before them stood the same man I had just seen in the cellar.

I looked around me at the boys – earnest, eager, tired faces, starved of fresh air and sunlight. As I stared, they seemed to change before my eyes. To change into adults, emaciated men whose bones pierced their unhealthy-looking skin. Evil-looking numbers had been branded into their flesh – the numbers of Auschwitz, Buchenwald, Treblinka. I looked back at their teacher. He was speaking to them gently but with great authority. I took my place among those living skeletons, and listened as attentively as they.

He spoke without bitterness of their suffering, conjuring up memories of a better life before those numbers were burned into their arms. From their expressions I could see they were reliving the recollection of their homes, their families, their loved ones. Then he turned to the future.

'You all dream of the Messiah. You picture Him above in the heavens. But He is actually here, on this earth with you. You believe He is untouched by the agonies which beset you – that He is sheltered from harm, but in reality He shares your suffering, the sadness that surrounds you, the pain of the cudgels which smash into your faces. The deprivation you are made to undergo – engulfs Him, too. He encourages you not to despair. Let me tell you He has greater need of you than you of Him. Do not abandon Him. You must ensure that He is not the only one of His people to survive.'

That word reverberated round the entire room.

'Survive . . . survive . . . survive!'

The speaker paused and looked deeply at each and every one present. They had remained still and silent, mesmerized by that man who seemed to know the secret of why we came into this world and why we depart.

I opened my mouth to speak, I wanted to urge him not to stop, to continue inspiring us, to 'take us back where everything began, where the world lost its innocence and God lost His mask' – but no words came to my lips. It was as if he understood my need, for he addressed himself directly to me.

'God is eternal only because we make Him so. As the Good Book tells us, "By accepting suffering and death, man creates the eternity of His creator".

'When they take your father, your wife, your son – your despair is God's. "Why?" you will ask of Him. "Where is the logic in that?" What matters then, my son, is not that two and two make four – that is logical – but that God is One. Only then will you realize what I have learned: that survival is not only essential – it is possible!'

The others turned to stare at me. Their death-like eyes pierced the very core of my being, and fear suddenly drenched me in sweat.

I cried out, 'Don't stare at me, I don't belong here, I'm not one of you, you all died in the gas chambers ... I'm alive ... I'm not ashes ... not dead ... not dead ... not dead! I'm not here ... not here ... not here ... alive ... alive ... alive!'

My words choked me and I could no longer breathe. I clenched my fists and beat my forehead to drag myself from the nightmare. It was then that my brain seemed to burst out of me and past and present were confused so that I was no longer conscious of where I was nor in which time I existed. Only his face remained clear before me, gazing with deep compassion into my innermost self.

'Who are you? Who are you?' I asked as he began slowly to recede from my consciousness.

'My name is not important, but they call me Manasseh.'

I was aware of someone shaking my shoulder and I opened my eyes. The synagogue guide was standing before me.

'I'm sorry I was so long. They asked many questions. Do you want to see the ritual bath?'

I followed him like an automaton, not listening to his monotonous patter – my mind was with another. I interrupted his flow.

'Who is Manasseh?'

The guide stopped talking and looked at me intensely.

'You could not have known him. You are too young.'

'Who was he?' I insisted.

The guide was sad now and his eyes focused on the distance.

'Manasseh was our Hebrew teacher, a Talmudic scholar. During the war, when the Germans came for us, it was he who hid the Sifrei Torah – the Scrolls of the Law – to preserve him. And when we were carted off in cattle-trucks to the concentration camps, he took with him only his prayer shawl and phylacteries . . . and a handful of round stones, which he always collected. It was an odd habit of his. When they took Manasseh to the gas chamber, he gave me his stones and he said,

'"If you survive, remember that life is as round as these stones. You end where you begin. And you recommence where you have ended."

'You ask who was Manasseh? He was a saint. He kept alive our hope and our belief in man. I could have lived happily in Israel after the war, but I came back to the synagogue because I could not desert his memory,' he added, almost inaudibly, 'and out of a sense of guilt because I was spared and he was not.'

The guide seemed suddenly to be ashamed of having said too much.

'But why do you ask?' he said. 'How did you know about Manasseh? There's no one left here but myself to remember him.'

I looked down at the stone which still lay in my hand, and I closed my fingers over it to hide it from the other's view.

'I'm afraid I must go,' I said, and gave him some francs for his pains.

'Oh, merci . . . for the synagogue funds,' he murmured. 'Au revoir, Monsieur. Come again.'

Come again? I don't know that I dare.

There are times when I tell myself it was all a dream, a figment of my imagination, until I pick up that stone and feel its smooth round surface in my hand. Shall I ever forget Manasseh? I don't think I can.